MAYA ANGELOU

A Biography of an Award-Winning Poet and Civil Rights Activist

by Donna Brown Agins

Enslow Publishers, Inc.
40 Industrial Road
Box 398
Berkeley Heights, NJ 07922
USA
http://www.enslow.com

Original edition published as *Maya Angelou: "Diversity Makes for a Rich Tapestry"* in 2006.

Library of Congress Cataloging-in-Publication Data

Agins, Donna Brown.
    Maya Angelou : a biography of an award-winning poet and civil rights activist / Donna Brown Agins.
       p. cm. — (African-American icons)
    Includes bibliographical references and index.
    ISBN 978-0-7660-3992-6
    1. Angelou, Maya—Juvenile literature. 2. African American women authors—
Biography—Juvenile literature. 3. African American women civil rights workers—Biography—Juvenile literature. I. Title.
    PS3551.N464Z527 2012
    818'.5409—dc23
    [B]
                             2011024335

Future Editions:
Paperback ISBN 978-1-59845-395-9
ePUB ISBN 978-1-4645-1147-9
PDF ISBN 978-1-4646-1147-6

Printed in China

062012 Leo Paper Group, Heshan City, Guangdong, China

10 9 8 7 6 5 4 3 2 1

To Our Readers: We have done our best to make sure all Internet addresses in this book were active and appropriate when we went to press. However, the author and the publisher have no control over and assume no liability for the material available on those Internet sites or on other Web sites they may link to. Any comments or suggestions can be sent by e-mail to comments@enslow.com or to the address on the back cover.

Cover Photo: Writer Pictures/Graham Jepson via AP Images

CONTENTS

Chapter 1

IN THE
SPOTLIGHT

As an unwed single mother with few job skills and a two-year-old son to support, nineteen-year-old Marguerite Johnson found that interesting jobs that paid well did not exist.[1] Often, while she worked behind the counter at the Chicken Shack restaurant in Oakland, California, she dreamed of a better future.[2]

One evening, there was a knock at the door of her home. When she opened it, a short thin man introduced himself to her as R. L. Poole from Chicago. He was looking for someone who knew how to dance, he said. Some friends had given him her name.

Right away she thought that he was a talent scout for a chorus line or maybe a big musical.[3] Poole told Marguerite that he was a dancer from Chicago and that he needed a partner. Marguerite did not know any of the dances he named, but she wanted to show him that she had dancing skill. So she tried to do the splits. It was not impressive: One of her feet hit a gas pipe, the other caught on a table leg. Then, once she had achieved the position, Marguerite was stuck. R. L. Poole had to help her up. Even so, he hired her.

Poole began teaching Marguerite his tap-dance routine at a local rehearsal hall. Day after day, they practiced. Soon they were ready to go onstage.

The night of the first performance, the band played a loud introduction and the audience applauded as Marguerite and Poole pranced onto the stage. Poole immediately began tap-dancing and reached out for Marguerite—but she did not move. Marguerite stood rock-still in the middle of the stage.

Poole glided by her and once again held out his hand. Marguerite still did not move. When he tap-danced up to her and hissed, "Come on!" she stared blankly as if he were a total stranger.[4]

Poole put his arm on her shoulder and gave her a hard push. Finally, Marguerite started dancing. She twirled all around the stage. Her heels slapped the floor as she performed their tap routine along with every dance step she ever knew. R. L. Poole tried his professional best, but he could barely keep up with her. Even when the music stopped, Marguerite continued dancing until her partner put his arms on her shoulders and pulled her off the stage.

After the performance, Marguerite was winded, exhausted, and happy. Until that evening's show, she did not know what she wanted to do with her life. Despite that frightened, frozen time on stage, she now understood that performing would be part of her life's work.[5]

Several years later, Marguerite Johnson took the professional name Maya Angelou. Over the next forty years, Angelou would travel the world, not only as a dancer but as a singer, civil rights activist, poet, playwright, author, director, and actress. She would be awarded more than fifty honorary doctorate degrees. Her journey would not be an easy one. But she would not give in to failure or despair.[6]

In following her own unique artistic path, Maya Angelou went on to become one of the most respected literary figures in the last half of the twentieth century.

Chapter 2

DIFFICULT YEARS

Marguerite Ann Johnson was born on April 4, 1928, in St. Louis, Missouri. Her brother, Bailey, who was a year older, called her "Mya sister."[1] His nickname shortened into Mya, though everyone else called her Marguerite. At the time when Marguerite was a little girl, African Americans were treated badly, especially in the Deep South. Black citizens did not have the same rights and privileges as whites. Blacks were not allowed to live in the same neighborhoods as whites, attend the same schools, or even sit near white people on buses and trains.

Hoping to find work, Marguerite's parents, Vivian Baxter and Bailey Johnson, Sr., moved the family to Long Beach, California, when the children were small. But by the time Marguerite was three, her parents divorced. Neither parent could care for the children, so three-year-old Marguerite and four-year-old Bailey were sent to stay with their grandmother. The children were placed onboard a train with tags tied to their wrists that read, "To Whom It May Concern," along with their names and destination— "Stamps, Arkansas, care of Annie Henderson." The porter in charge of the children's cross-country trip left the train in Arizona. With their train tickets pinned to the inside of Bailey's coat, the two of them traveled the remainder of the way by themselves.

The children rode in silence until the train left the northern states. When they reached the southern states, other African-American passengers fed them potato salad and cold chicken.

Annie Henderson greeted Marguerite and Bailey when they arrived in Stamps. Like many towns in the South, the small town of Stamps was divided by the railroad tracks into two separate parts: a black section and a white section.[2]

Their grandmother, whom the children called "Momma," lived at the back of the William Johnson General Merchandise Store with her son, the children's uncle Willie. As a baby, Uncle Willie had been dropped by a babysitter. The injury left him physically handicapped.

Over the next few years, Momma created a strict and sheltered environment for Marguerite and Bailey. Their lives revolved around the store, school, and church. Uncle Willy drilled his niece and nephew on multiplication tables and had them recite passages from the Bible.

The Ku Klux Klan (KKK)

The Ku Klux Klan was organized in 1865 in Pulaski, Tennessee, by six Confederate soldiers. Its members, all white men, were bound by a secret oath. The Klan quickly grew into a terrorist organization. Klansmen hid their identities behind masks, white robes, and high pointed hats. The Klan promoted itself as pro-American, which to them meant anti-black, anti-Jewish, and anti-Catholic. With their goal of keeping African Americans from having any rights in white society, the Klan was responsible for much of the racial violence that spread throughout the South. The Klan terrorized, lynched, or murdered many African Americans and those who sympathized with them. The KKK still exists today.[3]

One afternoon, when Marguerite was tending the pigs near the store, the town sheriff rode up on his horse and told the family that earlier in the day, a black man had "messed with a white woman."[4] He did not say exactly what had happened, but in those days a black man in the South could be attacked even for making a random comment to a white woman. The man alerted Marguerite's grandmother that the Ku Klux Klan planned to ride though the county that night, putting all black men in danger. He warned her to hide Uncle Willie.

Marguerite, Bailey, and Momma rushed into the store and emptied a bin of potatoes and onions. They helped

Uncle Willie struggle into the bin, then covered him with the vegetables. Momma prayed all night long. The Klan did not ride into their yard that night. But Marguerite never forgot the fear and anger she felt over that incident.[5]

The years passed. Marguerite and Bailey did not hear from either of their parents. During these years, Marguerite grew even closer to Bailey, whom she looked up to not only as a brother, but also as a companion and a protector. Marguerite believed that Bailey was as handsome as she was homely. She thought she looked tall and gangly while Bailey was small and graceful.

When relatives or friends said unkind things about Marguerite's looks, Bailey stood up for her. Marguerite and her brother enjoyed each other's company so much, they spent most of their time together.[6]

In 1933, when the children had lived in Stamps for three years, they received gifts from their parents. When Marguerite opened her gift—a tea set and doll—she ran out of the house, sat behind a tree, and cried.

The gifts brought up unanswered questions. She had often wondered why she and Bailey had been sent away. Did they do something wrong? Was it her fault? Marguerite struggled with these feelings all though her childhood.[7]

One year later, her father arrived in Stamps without warning. Her well-spoken father was tall and handsome. He was proud of Bailey and seven-year-old Marguerite. Each day the store filled with people who came to see Momma's son, "Big Bailey."

Marguerite's father stayed in Stamps for three weeks. At the end of that time, he said he was taking the children back to California with him. Marguerite was not sure she wanted to go, but she did not want to stay in Stamps without Bailey. Partway through the trip, their father told the children that he was not taking them to live with him in California. Instead, they were on their way to St. Louis, Missouri, to stay with their mother.

Marguerite cried when she realized she might never go back to Stamps to live with Momma. And she was panicked about seeing the mother she had not seen in four years.[8]

The instant she saw her mother, Marguerite decided that Vivian Baxter, with her light brown skin and her wide smile, was the most beautiful woman in the world. Marguerite then decided that she knew why her mother had sent her away: Vivian Baxter was too beautiful to spend her time looking after children. Big Bailey stayed for a few days, then left St. Louis for California.[9]

Life in St. Louis, with its tall buildings and paved streets, was very different from small, rural Stamps. Marguerite and Bailey lived in a big house on Caroline Street with their mother, their grandmother Baxter, and three uncles: Tutti, Tom, and Ira. The children were enrolled in Toussaint L'Ouverture Grammar School. They had done so much reading and studying in Stamps that they were academically ahead of the other students in the school.

In those days, the African-American section of St. Louis was a new and wild place. People sold illegal whiskey and lottery tickets in the streets. Many of these gamblers and bootleg whiskey salesmen were Grandmother Baxter's friends. Marguerite's mother worked as a card dealer in gambling parlors. Uncles Tutti, Tom, and Ira carried guns and often beat up people who disagreed with them. The adjustment to St. Louis was difficult for Marguerite and Bailey. Marguerite often woke at night with nightmares, and Bailey began stuttering.[10]

They had lived in the house on Caroline Street for six months, when Marguerite and Bailey moved with their mother and her boyfriend, Mr. Freeman, into a new house. Freeman worked in the Southern Pacific railroad yards. Some nights, when Marguerite had nightmares and could not sleep, she would crawl into bed with her mother and Freeman.[11]

One spring morning, when both Bailey and Vivian Baxter were not home, Freeman raped eight-year-old Marguerite. He threatened that if she told anyone, he would kill Bailey.[12] Then he sent her to the public library. Marguerite found it painful to walk, so she came home and crawled into bed.

During those first few days after being molested, Marguerite suffered terrible physical pain. She also felt guilt and confusion. Marguerite was young and did not understand that adults who abuse children are breaking the law. She blamed herself for what had happened. Freeman's threats against Bailey added to her terror.[13]

Marguerite stayed in bed for several days. She had trouble eating. Finally, Vivian Baxter said she was going to bathe

Marguerite and change the bed sheets. But the young girl fought her mother when she tried to lift her out of bed. When Vivian Baxter figured out what had happened, she took Marguerite to the hospital. Bailey cried when Marguerite told him that she had been raped. Then he told Grandmother Baxter, who called the police. Freeman was arrested.

Eight-year-old Marguerite testified at Freeman's trial. He was declared guilty and sentenced to prison for one year and one day. His lawyer arranged for Freeman to be released for the afternoon to make arrangements before he began serving his sentence. Later that day, a policeman came to Grandmother Baxter's house to tell her that Freeman had been found kicked to death in a vacant lot.

Even though she had nothing to do with his death, Marguerite felt that Freeman had died because of what she said in court.[14] She worried that she had done something to deserve the pain Freeman had caused her. She was too young to understand that none of this was her fault. In her view, her testimony led a man to his death.[15] This had a powerful effect on Marguerite. She feared that if she spoke, her words would cause harm. Marguerite decided not talk to anyone but Bailey.[16]

Marguerite did not speak for the next five years. At first her family accepted her silence. They understood she was upset. But after a while Marguerite's behavior annoyed them, especially after a doctor told the family that she was healed. Soon her relatives began spanking her for not answering when they spoke to her. Finally, something good came out of the terrible incident. Marguerite and Bailey were sent back to Stamps to live with Momma.[17]

The quiet and calm of Stamps proved to be good for Marguerite. The townspeople accepted the child's silence. She went to school and did her homework, but she never spoke in class.

One day when Marguerite was working in the store, a woman named Bertha Flowers came in to buy groceries. Well-educated Bertha Flowers was considered the aristocrat of black Stamps. She dressed beautifully, wore gloves, and spoke perfect English. Marguerite carried Bertha Flowers's groceries to her house, where the woman served Marguerite tea, cookies, and lemonade.

That afternoon was the first of what Mrs. Flowers and Marguerite called her "lessons in living."[18] Marguerite's new friend talked to her about the importance of written words and the power of the spoken word. Bertha Flowers had read many books and shared her love for reading and learning with Marguerite.

During other visits, she read to Marguerite and lent her books, then asked Marguerite to memorize and recite passages from the books. Reciting poetry became a way for Marguerite to speak aloud. It helped her begin talking with people again. The books, poetry, and conversations with her new friend had a positive effect on Marguerite.[19]

Over many months, Marguerite began to feel more confident, and at the age of nine she started writing her own poems. She attended the Lafayette County Training School, and did well. Four years later, in 1940, twelve-year-old Marguerite graduated from eighth grade at the top of her class.

Marguerite's eighth-grade graduating class joined the high school seniors for the commencement ceremony. Edward Donleavy a white political candidate running for office in Texarkana, Arkansas, addressed the audience of African-American parents and students. A graduation speech is usually an encouraging and inspiring message to the graduates. But instead of giving the young people a positive view of the future, Donleavy's graduation speech stressed to the all-black student body that they were not equal to whites. He reminded them that they would have few educational and professional opportunities in white society. Marguerite twisted her handkerchief and stared at her hands while she listened to him tell how she would be limited to low-level jobs or work that did not require an advanced education.

But as the graduating class sang "Lift Every Voice and Sing"—the African-American national anthem by James Weldon Johnson—Marguerite remembered that African Americans had suffered many tragedies and disappointments but had still triumphed.

Despite the speaker's discouraging words, Marguerite left the graduation ceremony with a sense of pride and hope for the future.[20]

Chapter 3

DAYS OF CHANGE

Atfter her 1940 graduation from Lafayette County Training School, Marguerite worked in the store during the week, and went to church every Sunday. One day, Uncle Willie sent Bailey on an errand in the white part of town. Bailey returned upset and shaken.[1] On his way home he had seen some white men pulling a body wrapped in a sheet out of a pond. The men unrolled the fabric by kicking the corpse. Then they ordered Bailey and several other African Americans to grab the corners of the sheet and carry the man's remains to the nearby jail. The white men threatened to lock them up with the dead body. The African Americans talked them out of it, but the event so upset Bailey that he spent the evening asking Uncle Willie why white people hated black people so much.[2]

Momma tried to explain, but her answers did not calm Bailey. She did not tell the children that the black man had been lynched, or that, because Bailey was becoming a young man, he was no longer safe in Stamps. This incident changed Marguerite's life once again. Momma packed some clothing and planned their trip to California.

Momma, Marguerite, and Bailey traveled by train to Los Angeles, where they stayed in an apartment. Six months later, their mother, Vivian Baxter, took Marguerite and Bailey to her home in Oakland, a city outside San Francisco.

Marguerite was now living in a strange city with the mother she had not seen for five years. She was so frightened that if she could have, she would have gone back to Stamps with Momma—even leaving Bailey behind.[3] Worse, her mother had recently remarried. There had been so many difficult experiences and changes in her life, Marguerite did not trust the relationship to be safe and secure.

Fortunately, her stepfather was kind and loving, and was a strong father figure to Marguerite and Bailey. They called him Daddy Clidell. Marguerite felt a sense of belonging with him. Daddy Clidell never had children of his own, and he was delighted to accept Marguerite as his daughter.[4]

At first, their mother, who still worked as a card dealer, seemed nervous around Bailey and Marguerite.[5] But as time passed, the children found Vivian Baxter unpredictable and fun. Once, she woke them up at 2:30 in the morning for a little party—just the three of them. Marguerite and Bailey were not pressured to study hard in school. Instead of going to church on Sundays, they went to the movies.

Daddy Clidell and Vivian Baxter bought a large boardinghouse in San Francisco. The family moved into part of the bottom floor and rented out the other rooms.

Marguerite was thirteen in 1941, when the Japanese bombed the naval base at Pearl Harbor, Hawaii, drawing the United States into World War II. For Marguerite, one of the greatest impacts of the war was the disappearance of Japanese citizens from the city of San Francisco. The United States government removed many Japanese Americans from their homes during the war.

Japanese Americans and World War II

Because the United States was fighting against Japan, Americans did not trust people of Japanese descent who were living in the U.S. During this time, more than 110,000 Japanese people, most of them American citizens, were forced to leave their homes, businesses, and all their possessions and move to remote areas of California and other states. Though they had not committed any crime, they were sent to live in relocation or internment camps until the war ended.[7]

As the Japanese-American population shrank, many African Americans moved into San Francisco from the southern states. They found jobs in shipyards and factories, and in many of the businesses that were formerly owned by Japanese families.

Marguerite knew racism festered below the surface of the city.[6] But as a thirteen-year-old newcomer, she enjoyed exploring San Francisco's streets, parks, and fancy buildings. Her mother often took her and Bailey to Chinese, French, and Italian restaurants. The children ate Hungarian goulash and Irish stew. Through food, Marguerite learned about other cultures and people.

Marguerite attended a school where she was one of three African-American students. Although she had always been smart, the other students had larger vocabularies and were not shy about actively participating in class. Miss Kirwin taught social studies and current events. Marguerite enjoyed the class because Miss Kirwin treated all her students with respect and stimulated her students to think independently.

At the age of fourteen, Marguerite received a scholarship to the California Labor School, where she studied drama and dance. Marguerite had always enjoyed music and drama. Now she had a chance to develop her talent.

The summer of her fifteenth year, Marguerite's father invited her to visit him in San Diego, California. From the start, there was friction between Marguerite and her father's girlfriend, Dolores Stockland. The two young women were very close in age but had little in common. Dolores was a quiet, tidy, petite perfectionist. Carefree, six-foot-tall Marguerite did not have any housekeeping skills. Things grew very uncomfortable between them, and Marguerite's father did nothing to help the situation.[8]

One night when Marguerite's father went out, she and Dolores had a physical fight. Marguerite was cut on the hand. Her father immediately arranged for her to stay with some friends. But Marguerite did not want to stay with people she did not know, nor did she want to go back to her father's home. So she left and wandered out into the streets of San Diego. After walking for a while, she found a junkyard and settled into an abandoned car for the night.

The next day she met other homeless teens who were living in the junkyard. Marguerite made friends with this community of teenagers. They lived by rules that they created themselves. They shared food and money earned from odd jobs. Marguerite appreciated their acceptance and felt a sense of belonging. But after six weeks of living as a runaway, Marguerite wanted to go home. She called her mother, who sent her a ticket back to San Francisco.[9]

Marguerite returned home to learn that her mother did not approve of Bailey's rough friends. A rift had developed between mother and son. The two fought continually. Marguerite did not take sides, but she was sad when Bailey finally moved out of their house.

Like many teenagers, Marguerite wanted to earn money. In the fall of 1944, sixteen-year-old Marguerite became the first black streetcar conductor for the Market Street Railway Company. She had told her new employers that she was nineteen.

By that spring, she had lost interest in school. And her deep voice and towering height distanced her from her classmates. Marguerite briefly became involved with a boy who lived nearby. They spent the night together once, and she became pregnant.[10]

Worried that her pregnancy would bring shame on the family, Marguerite decided not to tell anyone. On the night that she graduated from Mission High School in June 1945, she left Daddy Clidell and her mother a letter telling them she was pregnant. Once they got over the surprise, they insisted that she and her baby live with them. That summer, her son, Clyde Bailey Johnson, was born.[11]

Marguerite, only seventeen, was a child herself in many ways, but she did her best to take care of and support Clyde. At different times she had jobs as a waitress, dance partner, fry cook, secretary, and bar maid. No job lasted very long.

Just before she turned nineteen, Marguerite decided to join the army, where she could learn a trade and receive the benefits of the GI bill. The GI bill provides loans for veterans to buy a home and money to pay for school. The army accepted her, but one week before her induction, she was rejected. The California Labor School, where Marguerite had studied dance and drama, was believed to be a Communist organization, therefore unacceptable to the army.

Communism is a political philosophy that promotes a classless society. In a Communist society, private ownership is abolished, and the manufacture of goods, as well as the goods produced, belong to everyone in the community. This political philosophy is generally thought of as the opposite of democracy.[12]

Disappointed and lacking direction, Marguerite took another job as a waitress. She spent her spare time in Melrose Records, a neighborhood music store, where she enjoyed listening to new jazz recordings. Louise Cox, the owner, was impressed with Marguerite's knowledge of jazz and offered her a job. At first Marguerite was suspicious. She had never worked for, or been friends with, a white person. But Louise Cox treated her with respect. After a few weeks Marguerite realized, for the first time, that some whites could accept black people as equals.[13]

One afternoon while Marguerite was working, Tosh Angelos, a white man of Greek descent, came into the store. Tosh, recently discharged from the U.S. Navy, worked at an electrical appliance shop. He enjoyed jazz as much as Marguerite did. Tosh also enjoyed spending time with Clyde, who soon became fond of his mother's new friend. Marguerite appreciated his kindness. But when she brought her new boyfriend home to meet her mother, Vivian Baxter warned her not to become romantically involved with or to marry a white man.[14] Marguerite ignored her warning. In 1952 Marguerite, age nineteen, married Tosh Angelos.

The small family lived in a large rented apartment. For a while, Marguerite was happily married.[15] She left her job and became a full-time mother to Clyde, spending her days cooking, cleaning, and playing with her son. Marguerite especially loved reading to him. On weekends the family went on picnics in Golden Gate Park and to the movies. But after a year, the couple's differences began to cause friction. Tosh had a strong personality and tried to control all aspects of Marguerite's life. She was deeply religious and spiritual, and he did not allow her to go to church. He also did not want to include her family in their lives. These restrictions put a great strain on Marguerite.

Tosh did not believe in God. Marguerite had been raised to think of herself as a child of God. Secretly, Marguerite began attending church. When Tosh found out that she had been lying to him about where she went on Sundays, their relationship became more strained.[16]

One day Marguerite became ill with back and side pains so severe she fainted and was hospitalized. An operation to remove her appendix led to complications. Marguerite remained in the hospital for several weeks. When she returned to their apartment, Marguerite told Tosh she wanted to go home to her grandmother in Arkansas. But Momma, Tosh told her, had died while Marguerite was in the hospital. Marguerite mourned her grandmother and did her best to make the marriage work, but a year later Marguerite and Tosh divorced. They had been married two and a half years.

Although Marguerite was relieved to be out of the relationship, her son Clyde was hurt and angry over the breakup. Marguerite spent time comforting and soothing her heartbroken son, but she had very little money to support them and needed to find work.[17]

Marguerite landed a job as a dancer in a local nightclub, the Garden of Allah. After her performances, she sold drinks to the customers and was paid a percentage of what they spent. Although it was against the rules, Marguerite told the customers the amount of 7-Up and ginger ale that the bartender used to water down their mixed drinks. Soon Marguerite was selling more drinks than any of the other waitresses and became the most popular dancer at the club.[18]

One night four customers came to the Garden of Allah to watch Marguerite's act. One, a woman named Jorie Remus, performed at the Purple Onion, a famous club in San Francisco. Another, Barry, managed the club. They enjoyed Marguerite's show and invited her to sit with them afterward. Soon they were coming to the Garden of Allah regularly, and Marguerite became friends with them.

At the same time that Jorie was about to close her act and move to another club, Marguerite was fired from her job at the Garden of Allah because the other waitresses had become jealous of her success.[19] Jorie arranged for professional voice and dance coaches to help Marguerite put together a new routine of calypso music. Marguerite learned how to glide onto the stage at the beginning of her act and how to cue the piano player to begin playing for the most dramatic impact. Barry signed Marguerite to a three-month contract performing as a Cuban calypso singer at the Purple Onion. He suggested that she change her name to something more exotic. She decided to use her childhood name, Maya. For added dramatic effect, she changed her married name, Angelos, to Angelou.

As Maya Angelou, professional calypso singer and dancer, she had now taken a new path.

Chapter 4

NEW PATHS

For her opening night at the Purple Onion nightclub, Angelou had designed beautiful costumes with long flowing tops and skirts slit up the sides. Before performing, her knees felt weak and her stomach throbbed, but when her act opened to applause, Angelou walked onto the stage, calmly nodded to the pianist, and sang.[1]

Angelou's calypso act became popular. After several weeks of performances, newspaper reporters asked Angelou for interviews. She made guest appearances on radio and television. There was even a ten-member Maya Angelou fan club. Angelou enjoyed the popularity from her job at the Purple Onion. For the first time, her life had a stable routine. She spent her days with Clyde and spent her evenings onstage.[2]

In 1954 Leonard Sillman's Broadway hit show *New Faces of 1953* debuted in San Francisco. Angelou went to see it with the new Purple Onion manager, Don Curry. She enjoyed the musical and was impressed with the quality of talent.[3] Several weeks later, some members of the cast came to see Angelou's show and told her that one singer was leaving *New Faces of 1953*. The producer was auditioning dancer/singers to take her place. Angelou tried out and was offered the job. Excited, Angelou went to tell Don Curry that she was taking a role in *New Faces of 1953*. When Curry refused to let her out of her three-month contract, Angelou had to turn down the opportunity.

At the end of her contract, Angelou signed on for another three months at the Purple Onion. During this time, Angelou developed her own original material for the show. She composed music from poems she had written years earlier and wrote new songs to fit calypso rhythms.

One night, the Purple Onion was filled with people from the cast of the Broadway show *Porgy and Bess,* by George and Ira Gershwin. Angelou had taken Clyde to see the show. The story of the male lead, Porgy, and his love interest, Bess, moved Angelou. *Porgy and Bess* also had the greatest gathering of African-American talent that Angelou had ever seen.

After her performance, Angelou spent some time chatting with the cast members. They told her how much they liked her show. She enjoyed their company and felt a sense of belonging. She was impressed with the professionalism and loved the friendship and spirit of the group. The performers told Angelou there was an opening for a singer.[4] Angelou tried out for the part. Again she got the job, but she knew the manager of the Purple Onion would not let her out of her contract.

Three days before her contract was to run out, Angelou received a call from a Broadway producer. He was looking for a singer/dancer to play opposite Pearl Bailey, a famous actress. He asked Angelou to travel to New York for an audition. She did not want to leave San Francisco. But her mother and aunt told her they would care for Clyde while she was away. Angelou tried out and was offered a part in the play *House of Flowers*. Soon after Angelou shared the news with her family, the phone rang.

It was Bob Dustan, the business manager of Breen's Everyman's Opera Company. He offered Angelou the role of Ruby in *Porgy and Bess*. The company, then performing in Montreal, planned to leave for Italy in four days. They would visit twenty-two countries. Angelou turned down the part in *House of Flowers* and accepted the part in *Porgy and Bess*.

Her decision was not without inner turmoil and sadness. Twenty-six-year-old Angelou knew she would have to leave her nine-year-old son with her mother. Angelou remembered her own childhood, when her mother had left her for long periods of time. Now she was planning to leave Clyde with her mother. It was a painful decision to make. Angelou did not want to leave her son. But she had to work, and it would be good experience for her. She resolved that someday she would take Clyde to all the places that she was going to see.[5]

Later that week, in the fall of 1954, Angelou arrived in Montreal, Canada. The show's cast welcomed her. The first night Angelou watched the production from the sidelines. Rehearsals started the next day. The dance movements were easy for her, but Angelou had difficulty singing the songs in the proper key. She practiced the tunes again and again until she could sing them perfectly.

Angelou spent her mornings exploring Montreal. She knew from her history lessons that Canada was the final destination of many runaway slaves. For that reason, she felt Canadians were not as prejudiced as Americans.[6]

After performing in Montreal, the group of sixty adult performers and two child actors left Canada and traveled to Venice, Italy. Other than Canada, Angelou had never been out of the United States. She vowed to learn the language of every country the tour visited.

The opening night of *Porgy and Bess* was a success. The Italian people could have been a difficult audience to please, as they knew and loved opera. But they were impressed, and the company stayed in Venice for one sold-out week. Angelou played her part well and gained the respect of the other cast members. From the triumphant opening in Venice, the performers traveled to Paris. French audiences were so enthusiastic that the troupe extended its original three-week stay to several months.

One evening after performing in *Porgy and Bess,* Angelou went to the Mars Club, a nightspot that featured black entertainment. Angelou was asked to sing. She was so successful, the manager offered her a job. She had to say no because *Porgy and Bess* did not end until 11:30 at night. But the Mars Club's owner arranged for Angelou to arrive at 12:30. Several weeks later, another club owner who heard her sing offered her a job. After singing in the midnight show at the Mars Club, she rode a taxi across town to do another show at the Rose Rouge Club.[7] Angelou felt so guilty about leaving Clyde that she sent all the money she made home to her mother.

Angelou found that the French people's attitude toward race was different from that of Americans. There was never the threat of lynchings or violence against blacks, nor were they ever denied service in any restaurant, hotel, or bar in the country. As a result, several African-American entertainers had moved to Paris. At first Angelou thought Paris would be a good place for Clyde to grow up, and she seriously considered moving there. But one night, after she experienced racial prejudice from a wealthy French woman, she decided there was no real benefit to moving to France after all.

Because of political differences and the Cold War, the atmosphere in Yugoslavia was tense.[8] Performers were told not to wander more than four blocks from their hotel. When the company did go out, crowds gathered around Angelou and the other entertainers. Yugoslavian citizens had rarely seen a black person. Although the musical was well received in Yugoslavia, the members of the company were happy when they left behind the political tensions and the cold, gray weather.

The troupe then traveled to North Africa. Angelou was eager to see Egypt. Gamal Abdel Nasser, the president of Egypt, had skin as dark as Angelou's. Many people in Egypt had deep brown complexions, and for once Angelou did not feel she was a minority. The time Angelou spent in North Africa made her think about her people's past, and the history of slavery.[9]

The Cold War

In the 1950s, the United States and the Soviet Union had an uneasy peace. The two political superpowers did not engage in warfare, but the chilliness that existed between the nations because of their political differences was called the Cold War.[10]

Countries that had Communist governments, or countries that were linked to the Soviet Union, were considered Iron Block countries. An imaginary divider, called the Iron Curtain, walled off these countries from nations that practiced democracy. When the production of *Porgy and Bess* moved on to Yugoslavia, they were the first American performers to go behind the Iron Curtain.

The performers traveled from Egypt to Athens, Greece, then on to Israel, Spain, and Italy. *Porgy and Bess* was the first American opera sung at La Scala, in Milan, Italy—the most famous opera house in the world.

By the time the company reached Rome, they were tired. They had been on the road over a year. While she was in Rome, Angelou received a letter from her mother with disturbing news. A casino for African Americans had opened in Las Vegas and Vivian planned to become a dealer there. This meant there was no one to take care of ten-year-old Clyde. Worse, her son had come down with a severe rash that did not respond to medical treatment.[11]

Angelou wanted to resign immediately. But the show's business manager explained that if she left on her own, the company would not pay her fare home. In addition, she would be held responsible for paying the transportation costs for her replacement in the show. Angelou did not have enough money to do that.

Angelou appeared nightly in *Porgy and Bess,* and during the day she gave dance classes in African movement. Finally, two months later, she had enough money to book return passage on a ship to the United States. After several weeks of traveling by boat, train, and automobile, Angelou arrived in San Francisco.

When he saw her, Clyde jumped into her arms and did not leave her side. Angelou's mother welcomed her by heaping praise and affection on her. Angelou spent the first day giving gifts and telling stories about her time away.

But mostly she talked about how much she missed Clyde. Angelou also learned that her beloved brother, Bailey, was serving time in prison for selling stolen goods.

Clyde, who had once been outgoing, had grown quiet and withdrawn. His skin was raw and scaly. Angelou took Clyde to the dermatologist, then to an allergist. Nothing helped. Angelou felt guilt that in her absence this had happened. She blamed herself for his poor health.[12] Terribly upset over Bailey's imprisonment and Clyde's illness, she talked to a counselor. But the session did not give her much comfort. In the end she realized that she had to forgive herself. Angelou then made the decision that from then on, she would not take a job if it meant separation from Clyde.

Angelou spent the next few weeks with Clyde. They had picnics in Golden Gate Park and went to the movies during the afternoon. Clyde's rash slowly healed, and his appetite returned. The medicines did not work, but his mother's love did. As Clyde grew to trust that Angelou would not leave him again, he became talkative and expressed his opinions about everything.[13]

One day he told Angelou he had changed his name and would no longer answer to the name Clyde. Angelou told him about the beautiful and powerful River Clyde in Scotland. He answered that Clyde was a good name for a river, but not for a boy. It took a month for Angelou and the rest of the family to get used to calling him Guy.

When Angelou's agent found her a singing engagement in Waikiki, she took Guy with her. Both of them enjoyed the blue sea and the jasmine-scented night air of Hawaii. When they returned to San Francisco they lived on a houseboat in Sausalito for a year. But soon Angelou became restless. She knew her singing career would advance only if she lived in a place with an active professional music community.

In 1956, Angelou and Guy packed their things and moved to the Laurel Canyon area of Los Angeles. During that time, Angelou met the writer John Killens, a member of the Harlem Writers Guild, a talented group of African-American writers who met regularly to read and critique one another's work.

He read Angelou's writing and told her she had talent but needed to polish her work. He suggested she move to New York and join the Harlem Writers Guild. Angelou liked the idea, but she had some reservations.[14] Since Guy's birth fourteen years before, Angelou and Guy had lived in five different areas of San Francisco, three areas of Los Angeles, and in Hawaii. Guy had moved so often that it was difficult for him to make and keep friends. But Angelou could not resist the intense desire to belong to an artistic community of African Americans.

In 1957, Angelou and Guy moved to Brooklyn, New York. She did not have a job waiting for her or a place to stay. But twenty-eight-year-old Angelou felt that she had to trust life. She believed that life loved the person who dared to live it.[15]

Chapter 5

ON HER WAY

Angelou quickly found an apartment, enrolled Guy in school, and joined the Harlem Writers Guild. The meetings were held in John Killens's home. Although members did not pay dues or need membership cards, they were required to read from their own writing at their third meeting.

Angelou's hands and knees shook the first time she read aloud. When she finished, the other writers' reactions were so negative and harsh that Angelou could not move when the group broke for a snack. Her feelings were hurt until John Henrik Clarke, her toughest critic, explained that talent is not enough. Writing is hard work, and each sentence should be written over and over until it is perfect. Angelou decided she would work hard on the craft of writing and polish her work to become a good writer.[1]

Eventually, Angelou received encouragement, support and acceptance from the other members. Through the guild, Angelou made lasting friendships with intelligent and interesting people such as the writer James Baldwin and the comedian Godfrey Cambridge. Angelou also learned that many of the members were involved in the civil rights movement, which was beginning to grow across the country.[2]

To support herself and Guy, thirty-one-year-old Angelou performed at nightclubs on the Lower East Side of New York. Although she was writing all the material for her nightclub acts and had recorded six songs for Liberty Records, Angelou wanted to do more than entertain people. She wanted her work to make life better for African Americans.[3] Just before Angelou decided to quit singing and pursue a more meaningful career, the manager at the famed Apollo Theater offered her a week's engagement. She could not turn down the opportunity.

Angelou was honored to perform in the same theater where world-renowned musicians Dizzy Gillespie, Count Basie, and Duke Ellington had played. During rehearsals, the manager instructed Angelou not to close her show with her usual audience-participation song, "Uhuru." He explained that the audience was too sophisticated to join in a sing-along. Angelou did not listen to his advice; instead she followed her intuition.[4]

When Maya Angelou's first concert at the Apollo opened at one o'clock in the afternoon, there were about forty people in a theater that could seat seven hundred.

At first, the group did not respond enthusiastically to her performance, but midway through the show they warmed up to her voice. Angelou announced she was ending her act with the ballad "Uhuru." The word *uhuru* means freedom in several African languages.

Angelou told the audience that if they really wanted freedom from racial injustice, they must sing "Uhuru" along with her. Their loud response showed they were passionate about freedom. By the next evening, word about Angelou's show had spread through Harlem. Great numbers of people came to hear her perform and sing the song "Freedom."

But in the late 1950s, freedom was not just the title of a song. The civil rights movement, a movement seeking equality for all Americans, had taken hold in America. Every day the newspapers carried stories about brave citizens who risked their personal safety to change a system that judged a race of people as inferior because of the color of their skin.[5]

Inspired by the success of the Montgomery boycott, Dr. Martin Luther King called sixty southern African-American leaders to Atlanta and formed the Southern Christian Leadership Conference (SCLC). The SCLC dedicated itself to staging nonviolent demonstrations against civil rights violations.

In Arkansas, Angelou's home state, an angry group of whites surrounded nine black students trying to enter Little Rock's all-white Central High School in September 1957. The governor, Orval Faubus, called in the National Guard to stop the students from entering the campus. But President

Dwight D. Eisenhower issued an immediate order to end the blockage and authorized one thousand federal troops to accompany the students into the school.[6]

Mobilizing for Civil Rights

Angelou had grown up in the rural South and knew about segregation. The laws in many southern states required African Americans to sit in the rear of public buses, separate from the white riders up front. On December 1, 1955, in Montgomery, Alabama, an African-American woman, Rosa Parks, refused to give up her seat to a white man. When Rosa Parks was arrested, a Baptist minister in his late twenties, named Martin Luther King, Jr., led Montgomery's African Americans in a 381-day boycott of Montgomery's bus system. Many protesters were arrested. Violence erupted and bombs tore through four churches. Dr. King's home was bombed, too. Eventually the bus system was declared desegregated. Later, the United States Supreme Court ruled that separate public transportation systems were unconstitutional.[7]

One day after her act closed at the Apollo Theater, Angelou and Godfrey Cambridge went to a church in Harlem to hear the Reverend Martin Luther King, Jr. Dr. King spoke about the changes taking place in the South and throughout the country. He talked of achieving racial equality through peaceful marches, demonstrations, and boycotts. He encouraged the mostly African-American audience to face the distrust and hate of racial prejudice by turning loathing into love. Angelou listened carefully as Dr. King explained that by peacefully challenging racial injustice, African Americans would eventually achieve the many rights they had been denied for hundreds of years. He asked the audience for help and support. When Dr. King finished speaking, he led the group in singing "Oh Freedom."[8]

Angelou and Godfrey Cambridge were so inspired by Dr. King that they decided to put on a show to raise money for his organization.[9] Together they produced, directed, and performed in *Cabaret for Freedom*, a show made up of groups of African-American entertainers. Angelou called on her friends from *Porgy and Bess* to appear on stage. Cambridge found a director and arranged for the use of a theater in Greenwich Village. The money they charged for admittance paid the performers' wages—the rest was donated to SCLC.

On opening night, the audience included well-known Harlem politicians and famous African-American actors. The show received a standing ovation. *Cabaret for Freedom* ran the entire summer of 1960 and raised a large sum of money for Dr. King's organization. Angelou was sorry to see the show end, but at that point she was struggling financially. She had to find a job.[10]

A short while after the *Cabaret for Freedom* closed, Bayard Rustin, the northeastern coordinator for SCLC, chose thirty-two-year-old Angelou to replace him in that job. Her duties included fund-raising, coordinating volunteers, sending out mailers, and speaking on behalf of Dr. King's organization. Although Angelou did not have any typing or office skills, she believed in the cause and accepted the job.

During this time Angelou became engaged to Thomas Allen, a local bail bondsman. They had little in common, but Angelou imagined her life would be simple and calm if she married him.

One day after working in the SCLC office for several months, Angelou returned from her lunch break to find Dr. King waiting in her office. He made himself comfortable on the old couch and asked Angelou about her family. Angelou felt he had an easy friendliness.[11] She forgot that he was a well-known hero of the civil rights movement as she talked to him about growing up in the Deep South. Angelou told him about her brother, Bailey, who had never recovered from his wife's death and was serving time in prison for selling stolen goods. Dr. King was sympathetic.[12] Before he left the office, Dr. King thanked Angelou for the good job she was doing for the SCLC.

In addition to working for SCLC, Angelou was one of the founders of the Cultural Association for Women of African Heritage. This group of talented African-American women made themselves available to do performances or fashion shows for any organization that wanted to put on a fund-raising affair for SCLC.

One evening Angelou went to a gathering at John Killens's home and met an African freedom fighter named Vusumzi Make (pronounced Mah-kay) and called Vus.

He was from the Xhosa tribe in Africa and had been an attorney before escaping from South Africa and going into exile. The moment they met, both Angelou and Make were attracted to one another.[13]

Make, a member of the Pan-African Congress, was in America to petition the United Nations against South Africa's racial policy. Both Angelou and Guy were impressed with Make's knowledge of American history and his commitment to freedom for his people.

Though she was taken with Make, Angelou was engaged to marry Thomas Allen. Still, she had already been questioning whether or not she should marry him. The next time Angelou saw Vusumzi Make at a formal dance in Harlem, he grabbed her hand and insisted that he intended to change her life and take her to Africa.

Both men pursued Angelou by sending her gifts, notes, and flowers. Finally Angelou decided she wanted to explain to Make why she had decided to marry Thomas Allen.

They met in a bar near her home. But before Angelou could explain, Make proclaimed his love for her and pleaded so intensely that Angelou decided she wanted the life of adventure she would have with him. She had known him only a little over a week, but Angelou already cared for Make. She accepted his marriage proposal.

When Angelou told Allen that their engagement was off, he was angry and took back his gifts. In the end, she was happy with her decision and Guy was pleased that Make was going to be his stepfather.[14]

For the next several days, Angelou's friends held parties for the happy couple. At the end of the week, Angelou left her job at SCLC and traveled with Make to London. On the plane he took her hand and said that he was marrying her that very minute. Angelou agreed. They never formalized their relationship or spoke of marriage again.[15]

During that week in London Angelou met the other wives of freedom fighters. She told them about Dr. Martin Luther King, Jr., and listened to them speak about their native lands—Uganda, Somalia, and Ethiopia. Angelou shared stories about Harriet Tubman and how she had helped slaves escape to freedom.

At the end of the week, her husband went on to Cairo to take care of business. Angelou returned to the United States to find and furnish an apartment for her family. She was about to begin a new chapter of her life.

Chapter 6

EXOTIC
ADVENTURES

When Angelou's husband returned to the United States, he did not like the way she had decorated the apartment. Make replaced the thrift shop furniture Angelou had bought with new, more expensive pieces.[1] Over time Guy and his stepfather became devoted to one another, but Vusumzi Make was so finicky about having a perfectly clean home that Angelou felt that she had to dust and scrub constantly.[2] Make also insisted that the wife of an African freedom fighter did not work outside the home.[3] Angelou continued going to Monday-night meetings with the Harlem Writers Guild, but her days were spent cooking meals and straightening the apartment.

Angelou did not tell her friends of her dissatisfaction. Many of them had warned her not to marry a man she had known for less than a month. Cultural differences divided Angelou and Make, and as an independent, outspoken American woman,

Angelou had difficulty adjusting to her husband's insistence on being in command in the home.[4] But she thought his work was important, and because he was so kind to Guy, she put her own creativity and interests aside. Although she was not happy, she tried to make the marriage work.[5]

One day, while walking through Harlem, Angelou and her friend Rosa stopped to listen to a man named Malcolm X. In a furious, booming voice, he addressed the crowd gathered around him. He told African Americans about Elijah Muhammad, the founder of a religious movement called the Nation of Islam, also known as Black Muslims. Malcolm X's philosophy of civil rights and politics were the opposite of Dr. King's. Angelou had worked for Dr. King's organization, SCLC, which advocated love as a weapon to fight racial hatred. Malcolm X labeled whites "blue-eyed devils" and claimed that the white citizens of America were intent on black genocide.[6] Genocide is the deliberate killing, or extermination, of a race or religion by the ruling government.[7]

That afternoon there was something in Malcolm X's angry tone that attracted Angelou. While she did not follow the teachings of the Nation of Islam, she was filled with frustration and resentment over the unjust and often cruel treatment of African Americans in the United States.[8]

On the same day that Angelou heard Malcolm X, she received news that Patrice Lumumba, a freedom fighter in the African Congo, had been assassinated. He was a hero to blacks around the world. Angelou and other members of the Cultural Association for Women of African Heritage (CAWAH) wanted to show their sadness publicly. They planned to hold a small demonstration at the United Nations General Assembly. The women arranged to sit in the General Assembly room wearing mourning clothes with their faces veiled. Then, when the American ambassador, Adlai Stevenson, announced Lumumba's death, the women would stand.

The CAWAH members posted fliers about the demonstration at a prominent Harlem bookstore. The group did not expect more than fifty people to join them at the United Nations. Angelou was surprised to see several thousand African Americans gathered outside the building. Only a few people were allowed to enter the building. But the combination of demonstrators filling the streets and sidewalks, and the heavily armed police who surrounded them, made the atmosphere tense.

That evening Angelou and the others in CAWAH watched a report of the day's happenings on the news. Inspired by the crowd they had been able to gather, and wanting to do more, they went to Malcolm X and asked his advice about future events.

Malcolm X was supportive of the women but would not commit to helping them. He told Angelou he did not believe in peaceful public demonstrations or marchers chanting slogans of inequality.[9] CAWAH did not stage any more demonstrations, and eventually the organization disbanded.

In May 1961 thirty-three-year-old Angelou was offered a role of the White Queen in the off-Broadway production of Jean Genet's play *The Blacks*. At first her husband was

The United Nations

More than a half a century ago, the United States and its allies in World War II created the United Nations (UN). The charter of the United Nations states that the people of the world, through their representatives to the UN, would work toward resolving disputes by peaceful means and work out cooperative solutions to economic, social, cultural, and humanitarian problems.[10]

against her accepting the part. He argued that because she was the wife of a diplomat who was also a freedom fighter, it was undignified for her to be onstage. But after he read the script, Make decided it was important for Angelou to be in the show. The theme of *The Blacks* warned what could happen when people who are underdogs take control from the authorities. It speculated that once in power, the underdogs would behave in the same way as their oppressors. Angelou did not agree with that message. She felt that African Americans had learned humanity from their many years of suffering.[11]

Still, Angelou was happy to appear onstage again.[12] The play's talented cast included James Earl Jones, Godfrey Cambridge, and Cicely Tyson. The famous author James Baldwin visited the set often. Although Angelou enjoyed performing in the play, she demanded that the producers pay her for music she had composed for the show. They refused. Her husband sent an angry telegram to the producer. Angelou agreed with his action, but because of it, she was fired. When she left the play, she became aware of the family's worsening money situation.

This was a difficult time for Angelou. Sixteen-year-old Guy no longer asked his mother for advice. Instead, he turned to Make.[13] Often the two men shared jokes and secrets without explaining or sharing them with her. Though she appreciated the close stepfather-and-son relationship that Guy and Make shared, Angelou felt excluded. She also suspected that her husband was being unfaithful to her. Angelou began to withdraw from her friends and even from the Harlem Writers Guild.[14]

One day a final eviction notice was posted on their door. Her husband must have received the other warnings and hidden them from her, Angelou decided. She never knew how he made money or what his salary was. Upset, Angelou confronted him. In response, Make left the apartment. When he returned, he told Angelou he had sold their furniture and rented a furnished room in a hotel for the family. Then he left for Cairo, Egypt, to make arrangements for the family to move there.

After living in a musty, run-down hotel for three weeks, Angelou and Guy went to San Francisco to visit her mother. A few weeks later, Make sent Angelou and Guy plane tickets to Cairo. Angelou and Guy spent time exploring the streets of Cairo, enjoying the exotic sights and smells of the ancient city. They especially appreciated seeing so many dark-skinned people with good jobs and in positions of authority. Guy enrolled in school, quickly learned some Arabic, and did well in his classes.

Angelou spent her days cleaning and preparing elaborate dinners for African dignitaries. At first, she was content. But after several months, her housekeeper told her that bill collectors had been coming by for payments on past-due rent, furniture, and rugs. Wanting to help out financially, Angelou contacted an American friend, David Du Bois, who worked at the newspaper *The Arab Observer*. He arranged for her to get a job as an associate editor.[15]

Though Make strongly objected, Angelou took the job. Angelou convinced him that her working would allow him to spend more of his own money on helping exiles who had escaped from bad conditions in other African countries. He finally agreed. Angelou was the first woman hired in the *Observer* office, and only the second American.

During the year that Angelou worked at the *Observer*, she learned how to work with the layout artists, deal with typefaces, select a story to cover, and stay with it until she had gathered all the necessary information. Make helped her by sharing his political knowledge and understanding of Africa. But after a year at the *Observer*, Angelou still needed more money to make ends meet. In addition to working for the newspaper, she was hired by Radio Egypt to write commentaries for the broadcasters.

During this time, Angelou made lasting friendships with other women. One friend, Hanifa Fathy, was a poet. Another, Bhanti Williamson, was the wife of a Liberian diplomat.

Although she had good friends and interesting work, Angelou was lonely. Her husband traveled all the time, and teenage Guy remained busy with school and his own friends. Make worked constantly to locate friendly nations where newly escaped South African political refugees— who were now homeless citizens—could live. He also provided the recent escapees with clothing, food, and housing. Angelou admired her husband and appreciated the work he did, but by now she knew she no longer loved him. Often, even when he was in Cairo, he did not come home at night. One night, after another angry argument, Angelou told Make she planned to leave him.

Bhanti Williamson invited Angelou to the Liberian diplomatic residence after Angelou told her the marriage was over. Angelou had not expected to find a gathering there when she arrived. The chairs were arranged in a semicircle and people spoke in hushed tones. Then the confused Angelou saw her husband. A friend announced that the couple was going to participate in a palaver.

The traditional African palaver is a gathering of people brought together to discuss an important issue.[16] In this case, the palaver was being held to decide whether Angelou had good cause to end her marriage. Angelou objected, saying she had done nothing wrong and was not on trial. She was told that in order to live in Africa as an African, she had to participate. So she sat down next to her husband.

The group was divided. Half were assigned to defend Angelou, the others supported her husband. Angelou and

Make each told their side of the story. For Angelou, it was very difficult because she was not used to talking about private things in public. The members of the palaver finally decided that Angelou had the right to leave the marriage, but they asked her to give Make one more chance. Angelou agreed to stay with him for six more months.

The next two seasons passed slowly, as Angelou planned the future. Guy had graduated from high school while in Cairo. Mother and son now agreed that the University of Ghana would be a good place for him to attend college.

Angelou would help Guy get settled in his dormitory in Ghana. Then she would travel to Liberia, where friends had helped her find a job at the Department of Information.

Make bought Angelou and Guy plane tickets to Ghana and arranged for them to stay with friends of his in Accra. In July 1962, thirty-four-year-old Angelou and seventeen-year-old Guy were once again moving on to another new world.

Chapter 7

SEEKING HER HERITAGE

During the early 1960s when Angelou and Guy lived in Egypt, the United States was in a growing state of political and social unrest. Before the end of the decade, the tensions from hundreds of years of unfair treatment based on racial prejudice against African Americans would erupt in rioting in East St. Louis, Chicago, and Detroit.[1] Americans were struggling to make sense of the many violent events that filled the evening news. When President John F. Kennedy was assassinated in November 1963, the United States went into a state of mourning. Later that same year a bomb exploded in a church in Birmingham, Alabama, killing four innocent African-American girls. Also in 1963, civil rights activist Medgar Evers was shot in front of his home in Mississippi.[2]

By contrast, Angelou and Guy arrived in Ghana during a time of hope and optimism. Ghanaian President Kwame

Nkrumah, an African hero, was admired by black people all over the world.[3] Angelou and her son were pleased that in Ghana there was no discrimination based on skin color.

For the first time in their lives they were surrounded by people of their own color.[4] Qualified citizens of Ghana could hold whatever available job they wanted. As a group they were not relegated to being low-paid, unskilled workers.

By the time Angelou moved to Ghana, many black Americans had immigrated there and formed a community. This included Julian Mayfield, a friend from the Harlem Writers Guild, and the famous writer W.E.B. Du Bois.[5] The group was made up of teachers, farmers, American government personnel, businessmen, and those who were dedicated to Pan-Africanism.

Pan-Africanism

Pan-Africanism refers to a movement founded around the turn of the century. This movement worked to secure equal rights, self-government, and unity for African peoples. Pan-Africanism encourages the study of African history, culture, and leadership. Kwame Nkrumah was a leading figure in this movement.[6]

Angelou dubbed the group the "Revolutionary Returnists."[7] She felt right at home with her new friends. They encouraged her to stay in Ghana. But she had made a commitment to the Liberian Department of Information and was eager to settle Guy into his college dormitory and then move on to start her new job.[8]

They had been in Ghana for only three days when Guy was seriously injured in a car accident. Wrapped in a plaster body cast because of a broken neck, Guy floated in and out of consciousness. Angelou's shock and self-pity overwhelmed her. She forgot about her new friends and recent happiness. Day after day Angelou sat by her son's bedside and worried about Guy's injuries and her own future. During this difficult time, Angelou often drank too much alcohol. The friends she had been staying with lost patience with her miserable mood. They were relieved when Angelou rented a room at the local YWCA. Soon she began to run low on money.

Fortunately, a friend arranged an interview for Angelou. She was hired as an administrative assistant at the University of Ghana and was permitted to live in the house of a professor who was out of the country for six months. After one month, Guy was released from the hospital. Four months later, he had healed enough to start college.

Angelou had mixed feelings about Guy's moving into the dorm. She worried about his well-being and was sad that this would be the first time since he was nine that they would be living apart from each other. But Guy reassured her that he would be fine. Before she left his dorm room, Guy hugged his mother and said, "There's something I want you to remember. It is my neck and my life. I will live it whole or not at all. I love you, Mom. Maybe now you'll have a chance to grow up."[9]

Angelou moved from the professor's house into a pretty white bungalow with two other American women, Vicki Garvin and Alice Windom. Soon their home became the meeting place for many of the Americans living in Ghana.

But as much as Angelou and her friends admired Ghana, native Ghanaians did not feel the same way about them. Often the people of Ghana were unfriendly, suspicious, and scornful of the American foreigners.[10] Ghana had gained independence from Britain just five years before. When someone tried to assassinate President Nkrumah, the Russian and American citizens in Ghana became the first suspects. The accusation upset Angelou.

Although black Americans were considered outsiders by the citizens of Ghana, this did not stop Angelou from trying to fit into the culture. She dressed in long, flowing robes, wore traditional head wraps, and learned to speak Fanti, the native language of Ghana. On weekends Angelou liked to leave the bustling city of Accra and drive to the countryside.

Angelou had lived in Ghana for a year when she traveled to a gold-mining town called Dunkwa. On her way she stopped for gas in the town of Cape Coast. She knew the history of the Cape Coast castle and the nearby Elmina Castle. The massive buildings sat on top of huge dungeons. During the time of the slave trade, Africans were held there before being loaded onto slave ships and taken to America. Now the castles were tourist attractions. Haunted by the thought of the castle's past, Angelou quickly filled her gas tank, then sped out of town.

But soon Angelou began to weep. She was filled with pain as she thought about her ancestors. Sweat dripped down her face. Through her tears, the highway ahead looked unclear. Angelou pulled over to the side of the road. Visions of being captured, tied up, and sold as a slave filled her mind. She pictured African ancestors who had been stolen by brothers, sold by their relatives, then bought by strangers. There were no sounds in her visions, just huge clouds of sadness. Then Angelou shook with anger thinking about the once free Africans who had become slaves in a strange land across the sea. Later talking about that day, she said that history had invaded her car. After a while, Angelou stopped crying and continued her trip to Dunkwa.[11]

Before long, Angelou stopped in a small village. She could not find a hotel room, and she did not have enough gas to travel to the nearest large town. Angelou asked a woman who was walking by the side of the road if she knew of a place to stay. The woman took Angelou to a thatched hut. The family that lived there treated Angelou as if she were an expected guest. They fed her and tried to figure out Angelou's tribal origin. It was with these people that Angelou felt her first sense of belonging in Africa.

The next day, Angelou drove back to Accra and her job at the University of Ghana, where she was responsible for maintaining student records. In addition, she taught drama and dance. But the money she made from her job barely covered her rent and Guy's tuition. To make extra money, Angelou wrote commentaries on American racism for the *Ghanaian Times*.

In the spring of 1963, Angelou and her roommates were looking at a magazine and discussing Dr. King's upcoming March on Washington. By this time Angelou had changed her philosophy. Angry and impatient with the slow progress of the civil rights movement in the United States, she no longer believed that marches would change society. Even so, she and her friends decided to demonstrate in front of the American Embassy to show their support of black Americans.

Because of the seven-hour time difference, their demonstration began at midnight. As the sun came up, Angelou realized that the Revolutionary Returnists were the only ones there. Two marines guarded the embassy. One was African American. When the marchers asked him to join them, he ignored them. As the African-American soldier raised the American flag, Angelou realized that no matter where she was in the world, she would always consider the American flag to be her flag. Even though her people had been slaves in the United States and she disagreed with much of the politics and policy, America was her home.[12]

Guy's teenage years had been difficult for Angelou. Now Angelou and her nineteen-year-old son had a major disagreement over his dating a woman older than Angelou. Angelou knew if she talked to the woman, it would only make Guy angrier. Not knowing what else to do, Angelou decided to distance herself from Guy. The producer Sidney Bernstein had offered her a part in the play *The Blacks*. She accepted the role and traveled to Venice, Italy, to perform with her old friends from New York.

After the play closed, she joined some friends who were traveling to Cairo for a political conference. Angelou ended her stay in Cairo by attending a large formal dinner with the Egyptian president. She sang "Swing Low, Sweet Chariot" and other African-American spirituals at the dinner.

Guy seemed friendlier when she came back from Cairo. But just as Angelou was accepting their repaired relationship, Guy told her that he considered himself an independent man, and he wanted them to lead separate lives. Angelou was thrown off balance by his statement, and not sure how to handle it.

In 1964 Malcolm X came to visit the Revolutionary Returnees at Julian Mayfield's home. Angelou was among the group listening to Malcolm X tell about his pilgrimage to Mecca.[13] He said he had been transformed by what he learned there. He no longer preached hatred for white Americans. Instead, he now considered some white men to be brothers and friends.[14]

Malcolm X told the group that he wanted to meet and gain support from as many African leaders as possible. Then he planned to go before the United Nations to condemn the United States for its racist policies. Angelou and the other Revolutionary Returnees agreed with his plan and wanted to help him. Within their group they knew many cabinet members, ambassadors, and other African and European diplomatic leaders, including Kwame Nkrumah, the president of Ghana.

After his visit with the president, Malcolm X approached Angelou and asked her if she would come to work for his newly founded Organization of Afro-American Unity, in New York.

Angelou had long talks with Guy and her friends. She enjoyed living in Ghana but knew that the civil rights movement in the United States was important. She realized that Guy did not need her. When she told him she was considering moving back to the United States, his broad smile told her how he felt.[15] Angelou knew that Guy's independence would be easier for her to handle from a distance. Leaving Ghana to work for Malcolm X was the right thing to do.

But before leaving Africa, there was one more place she had to visit.

Chapter 8

WANDERING

Angelou wanted to see eastern Ghana before she returned to the United States. For the first several hours of the trip, Angelou and two other passengers relaxed in the backseat of a car and listened to the murmur of the engine. Red bougainvillea bloomed wild by the sides of the roads. Clusters of palm trees grew scattered over the hillsides.

Suddenly, as their vehicle approached a bridge, Angelou became tense.[1] She announced that everyone had to get out of the car. Puzzled, the passengers got out and walked across the bridge. Angelou did not know why she was so afraid to ride across the bridge in the car, but she knew it was a feeling she could not ignore.[2]

When she got back in, their guide, Mr. Adadevo, asked her if she knew anything about the history of the region. Angelou said no. He explained that the bridges in that area were known for being poorly constructed. Often, when there was a heavy rain, the platform could not hold the weight of a car, and only if people walked across would they arrive safely on other side.

Later in the East Ghana town of Keta, Mr. Adadevo guided Angelou toward the marketplace. He wanted her to meet his sister. When Angelou climbed the stairs to the open-air market, she saw a tall, thin woman standing at the top. The woman spoke to her in Ewe, the language of the region. Angelou shook her head. Even though she did not understand the villager's words, she noticed that the stranger's voice was similar to her own. The woman took Angelou by the hand and led her from stall to stall. The other villagers also refused to believe that Angelou was an American who spoke only Fanti and English.[3]

Mr. Adadevo translated that the women insisted she was someone else, someone they knew. Angelou showed them her California driver's license. The villagers' insistence turned to sadness, which puzzled Angelou. During the time of slavery, Mr. Adadevo explained, nearly everyone in the Keta village was taken away or killed. But a few children ran away and hid in the bush. These boys and girls watched from afar as their parents were put in chains and taken away while their village burned to the ground.

Angelou had come to Africa to find a missing piece of her identity. Here in the village of Keta on one of her last days on the continent, she connected to her people's land of origin. Now Angelou was ready to return to the United States. She knew her new job in New York with Malcolm X was important work, and she was eager to get started.

Several days later, at the airport in Accra, Guy and many friends gathered to say good-bye to her. Although Angelou's relationship with Guy was still tense, she told him that she had opened a bank account for him and paid his college tuition. He thanked her and said that he wanted to support himself as soon as possible.

Angelou landed in New York on Friday, February 19, 1965. She spent the night with her friend Rosa Guy, then spoke to Malcolm X before flying to San Francisco. Her mother met Angelou at the airport and hurried her to the car. During the time Angelou was away, her brother Bailey had been released from prison. Now, when Angelou opened the door, she was thrilled to see her brother in the backseat. He had traveled from Hawaii to see her. Angelou had not seen her family during the four years she lived in Africa, but their closeness was still intact. When Angelou entered her mother's house on Fulton Street, everything was exactly the same as she remembered.

Bailey and her mother were eager to hear about Guy. Angelou described how her son often broke dates with her, and no longer asked for or followed her advice. She told them how, once, when she went to his house for a surprise visit, Guy had said she was not welcome.[6]

She felt guilty returning to the United States without him, she announced, but had told Guy she was giving him his freedom—in fact, was giving him Ghana. Both Bailey and her mother understood Guy's need for independence. Angelou had been a mother since she was in her teens. She and Guy were rarely separated. Now, as a thirty-six-year-old woman, she accepted his separation from her as a natural stage in his development.[5]

Finding Her Roots

The women whose features were similar to Angelou's believed that Angelou was a descendant of a native of Keta who had been taken into slavery. When she heard that, Angelou wept with the women.[6]

She mourned for the sad and tortured history of her people. But Angelou also cried tears of joy. Despite the tragedy of slavery and their displacement to a new land, her people had survived. Angelou knew there was a lot to cry about, but also much to celebrate. Through many years of despair, unfair treatment, and slavery, her people had faced down disaster, and dared to hope.[7]

A day later, on Sunday, February 21, 1965, Malcolm X was shot while giving a speech at the Audubon Ballroom in Harlem.[8] His pregnant wife and four small daughters were nearby when the bullets struck and killed him.

Angelou was filled with grief and sadness. But she also experienced another emotion: curiosity. While living in Ghana she had heard that the mood of unrest in the United States was so strong that the African-American community was ready to riot against acts of injustice. Angelou could not understand why no one she spoke to about the assassination seemed to care very much. Days passed. There were no demonstrations, marches, or riots denouncing Malcolm X's assassination.[9]

Angelou talked to Bailey about her future. Now no job waited for her in New York. And she was not happy living in San Francisco. Bailey suggested that she move to Hawaii. When Bailey returned to the islands, he found her a job singing at the Encore, a nightclub in Honolulu. He also talked Aunt Leah, their mother's sister, into letting Angelou stay with her until she found a place of her own.

Several weeks later, Angelou was in Hawaii rehearsing with a rhythm section and working out her new act. Angelou had not performed in a nightclub for a long time, but the minute she set foot onstage, she felt at home.

One night, after living in Hawaii for a few months, Angelou went to hear singer Della Reese in a nearby nightclub. Angelou mentally compared her own voice to the velvet voice of Della Reese, with its powerful sound and beautiful phrasing. She could not compete, Angelou decided. She would have to find something else to do with her life. Before leaving Hawaii, Angelou heard from friends in Ghana that Guy had settled down and was becoming a confident young man. Friends in New York reported that Betty Shabazz, Malcolm X's widow, had given birth to twin girls.

After a great deal of thought, Angelou knew that, because of Malcolm X's death, she no longer wanted to have anything to do with politics.[11] She then chose Los Angeles as the place where she would begin her new life.

Angelou had come to Hawaii with a heavy heart. Now she would move to Los Angeles feeling better. She did not know what she was going to do in southern California, or where she was going to live. But once again, Angelou knew that "life was waiting on me and it wasn't wise to test its patience."[10]

Chapter 9

FINDING
MEANING

When Angelou arrived in Los Angeles in the spring of 1965, she contacted Frances Williams, a woman she had known a decade earlier. Williams helped Angelou find a place to live and a job. Angelou furnished her apartment with secondhand furniture and hung brightly colored posters on the walls. She went to work for Random Research—a marketing research firm that gathered information on what types of products people used in their homes. The job did not pay well, but Angelou could set her own schedule and that made it worthwhile. This allowed her the time to begin writing a play.

Angelou was assigned to Watts, a mostly African-American neighborhood in South Central Los Angeles. She remembered the area from ten years before as a tranquil neighborhood where children played on well-kept lawns. Angelou's job was to knock on doors and ask women what cleaning products they used. Her conversations always began with gathering this information, but usually ended with Angelou listening to the women's stories about money and family problems.

Day after day Angelou observed house after house where unemployed men idly sat on porches of run-down homes. She knew that many African Americans were angry and frustrated because they had lost their jobs. Because of unemployment, family frustrations, and lack of opportunities, the divorce rate in the area grew, and children were often left home alone after school. Angelou rarely saw kids happily riding bikes around the neighborhood. Instead, gangs of thugs roamed the streets of Watts.[1]

One late afternoon in August 1965, when Angelou was home working on her play, she smelled burning wood. The charred smell was followed by the odor of scorched food, then the stink of burning rubber. An hour later, Angelou's television broadcast the news of a full-blown riot in Watts. People's pent-up anger from years of racial inequality had exploded. The rioters threw rocks at police in cars and patrols on foot. She watched the news coverage showing groups of young men refusing to allow fire trucks into the streets to put out the fires.[2]

After two days of viewing the riots on television, Angelou drove to Watts. She walked down streets lined with overturned cars and burning buildings. She saw people who had held their frustrations and anger inside for too long. Now they were hauling shopping carts full of looted goods out of stores.

Sirens screamed all around her. Angelou stared at the police as they rushed around, helpless to stop the rioting.

Suddenly, police wearing riot gear and gas masks surrounded her. The air darkened, clouded with smoke. Angelou panicked and ran. After sprinting for nearly a mile, Angelou realized she had parked in the opposite direction.[3] She circled back, found her car, and hurried home. Over the next thirty-six hours, Angelou watched the news on television. The city jails began to fill. Hundreds of looters were arrested, but the rioting did not stop.

Rioting Against Racism

Televised throughout the nation, the Watts riots brought into focus the massive pattern of segregation in urban areas. The Los Angeles riot was the most costly and violent in modern American history. By the time the fifteen hundred National Guardsmen pulled out, 34 people had died, 4,000 were under arrest, and property damage totaled between $50 million and $100 million.[4]

Several days later, Angelou returned to the riot area. On her earlier visit, shop fronts had been charred on only a few streets. Now she saw burned-out buildings all over. This time, Angelou was determined not to run away. Before, she had seen rage in every face. Now there were areas of calm, and the violence had lessened. Political and community representatives formed committees to talk about problems and come up with solutions.[5]

City officials asked the citizens of Watts what they wanted or needed to help their community. Unemployed people said they wanted jobs. The underemployed wanted better jobs. The women of the area wanted an accredited, well-funded day care center. Another group wanted a medical center so the local citizens would not have to travel far to see a doctor. In time, as the negotiations progressed, the area would begin to rebuild.[6]

After the riots, Angelou went back to her market research job. She auditioned for and got a part in a production of the play *Medea*. Angelou also continued writing her own play, titled *All Day Long*. Her work told the story of a poor thirteen-year-old African-American boy who had relocated to the North after growing up in the southern United States. Among his many surprises were indoor toilets, the northern accent, and a couch that could open into a bed. Angelou had experienced the same surprises thirty years before, when, as a child of seven, she had moved from her grandmother's home in Stamps to her mother's house in St. Louis.

She showed the completed script to a friend. He told Angelou to find a theater, director, and producer. But she could not find anyone interested in producing her play. Never afraid of hard work or a challenge, Angelou went to the library to learn about becoming a producer herself. Angelou learned that, unfortunately, producing her own play would take more money than she had.

During this time, Kwame Nkrumah, the president of Ghana, was removed from power while he was on a visit to

China. In the past two years of Angelou's life, Malcolm X had been murdered, Watts had burned, and now, with Nkrumah out of power, Angelou knew she would never go back to Ghana.[7] Angelou decided to leave Los Angeles and relocate to New York. Just as she chose a departure date and arranged for housing, her doorbell rang. It was her brother, Bailey.

Bailey told Angelou that Guy had returned to San Francisco several days earlier. Guy had been sitting in a parked car that was hit by an out-of-control truck. Guy's injuries once again included a broken neck. Bailey had driven all night to reach Angelou. Panicked and upset, Angelou drove back to San Francisco with Bailey. Seven hours later, they arrived at their mother's house. Vivian Baxter drove Angelou to the hospital.

In spite of his injuries, Guy looked like a grown man to Angelou. Though she had not even been anywhere near her son, she still felt guilty that she had not protected Guy from the accident.[8] Angelou stayed with her mother for several weeks and visited Guy in the hospital every day. He had finished college in Ghana. He felt he had gotten all the country had to give. He told Angelou that he would find work, as soon as he was well. Angelou marveled at how her son seemed like a grown-up stranger who reminded her of her son.[9]

Guy planned to stay in San Francisco with his grandmother when he was released from the hospital. Angelou knew her mother would take good care of him. She felt comfortable going ahead with the move to New York.

Angelou moved into her friend Rosa Guy's apartment on the Upper West Side neighborhood of New York City. They shared expenses and cooking. For the next few weeks Angelou adjusted to the fast pace of life in New York and started working on her poetry. One afternoon she had lunch with an old acquaintance, Jerry Purcell, who owned an Italian restaurant and acted as an agent for some performers. Years earlier Angelou had entertained at a fashionable nightclub he owned. Though Angelou was no longer looking for work in the entertainment business, she thought he might help her find a job.

Angelou told Purcell that she was living with a friend and writing poetry, but she longed to write plays. Her problem was that her money was disappearing fast.

Purcell listened while continuing to greet customers at his restaurant. When Angelou said good-bye to him, he handed her an envelope. Angelou opened the envelope in the cab on the way home. Inside was a large amount of cash. For the next two years, Purcell helped Angelou financially and never asked for anything in return.

Soon afterward, Angelou moved into her own place on the Upper West Side. Although the apartment's style was more modern than she preferred, she had a view of Central Park from the living room window. Once again she furnished it with purchases from secondhand stores and estate sales. Weeks later she entertained a number of famous friends in her new home. James Baldwin and John Killens were friends from the Harlem Writers Guild. Julian Mayfield and his wife, Ana Luisa, had returned from Ghana. They, too, enjoyed Angelou's home cooking.

In 1968 Angelou went to a concert at Carnegie Hall to celebrate the one-hundredth anniversary of the birth of the writer, philosopher, and historian W.E.B. Du Bois, who had died in Ghana in 1963. The audience was silent with expectation as actor Ossie Davis, the master of ceremonies, introduced Dr. Martin Luther King, Jr. Seated with James Baldwin's family, Angelou listened to Dr. King speak about W.E.B. Du Bois. Dr. King told the audience that Du Bois had included people of all colors in his dream of a fair and workable future for the United States and the world.[10]

Afterward Angelou, along with James Baldwin, his mother, Berdis Baldwin, and his siblings, met Dr. King in the corridor of the theater. When Dr. King asked Angelou what she was doing now, she answered that she was writing a play. He told her he was expanding the nature of his organization, SCLC, to include issues related not only to race but to society as a whole. He explained to Angelou that he was organizing a Poor People's March on Washington, D.C. This march was not a black or white people's march, but a demonstration to bring attention to poverty in the United States.

Dr. King asked Angelou to travel around the country and to ask preachers if their churches would donate one Sunday's collection money to the Poor People's March. Angelou explained to Dr. King that her fortieth birthday was several weeks away. She agreed to help him, but not until after she had celebrated her birthday.

Chapter 10

IN FULL SWING

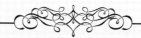

O n April 4, 1968, Angelou spent the day preparing for her birthday celebration that evening. She had always enjoyed cooking, and now she whipped up her favorite recipes: Texas chili without the beans, baked ham and candied yams, rice and peas, macaroni and cheese, and a pineapple upside-down cake. Angelou put vases of daffodils on the tables and cleaned the apartment until everything sparkled. After the buffet of food and drinks was set out, Angelou admired how festive everything looked. The ring of the phone startled her.

Her friend Dolly said she was coming right over and made Angelou promise not to turn on the television. Angelou wondered what could have happened that caused Dolly to be so concerned. When Dolly arrived at Angelou's apartment, she looked grief-stricken. Angelou tried to cheer her up. But Dolly interrupted: "Martin Luther King was shot. He's dead."[1]

At first Angelou did not believe her. When she finally realized Dolly was telling the horrible truth, she ran out of her apartment. Angelou's neighbor across the hall left his apartment at the same time, and they walked together to Harlem. On the way, Angelou could hear Dr. King's deep voice and messages of hope echo in her head.

People automatically gather together in grief when an important public figure dies. In Harlem, citizens had already poured into the streets and stood sobbing on the sidewalks. Strangers cried and hugged other strangers. As Angelou continued walking, all around her she heard men and women asking one another, "Why? Why?"[2]

A television in the window of a local appliance store played tapes of Dr. King. There was no sound, but people gathered in groups five and six deep in front of the shop window. Shocked and sad, Angelou stayed for a while, then walked on. As crowds of people rushed by, there were loud shouts and breaking glass. She went into a small diner and sat down. There was no service, but the owner told her to pour a cup of coffee from the pot.

Angelou put her head down on the counter. After a while a man spoke to her in a sad, quiet tone. He told her the rage in the streets was about Malcolm X. Angelou was surprised to hear Malcolm X's name. The man explained that Malcolm X had been shot not far from there, and at the time of his death there were no gatherings or memorials. The man said that the show of support in the streets of Harlem was partly for Dr. King, partly for Malcolm X, and partly for the many African-American leaders who had been gunned down.[3]

For the next few weeks Angelou was in a daze of sadness. At times she thought history was repeating itself. Pictures of Coretta Scott King, the widow of Dr. King, standing with her now fatherless children reminded Angelou of Jacqueline Kennedy standing with her children after her husband, President John F. Kennedy, was slain by an assassin's bullet. Over and over, Dr. King's name was linked with that of Malcolm X in the media. Angelou became so depressed she could hardly walk and she no longer wanted to talk. To gain balance, she decided to stay home for a few weeks. Her friend Dolly agreed that Angelou could stay in her apartment. But Dolly did not want Angelou to stop speaking, as she had after being traumatized as a young girl. Dolly insisted that Angelou call her once a day. Jerry Purcell sent an employee every day with a hot meal.[4]

Several weeks later, James Baldwin came by and told Angelou he was taking her out for the evening. He took her to the home of Jules Feiffer, one of the nation's funniest and most skilled cartoonists. Feiffer and his wife, Judy, welcomed both guests. The evening was filled with laughter and good food. At one point, Judy Feiffer told Angelou she should write her autobiography. Angelou told her she was not interested.[5]

Several days later Angelou had a meeting with two producers from the television station KQED in San Francisco. They spoke about wanting to hire someone to do a ten-part series on African-American culture and history. They had called Angelou because they knew she had lived in Ghana. They wanted an insider's view of Africa and America. Angelou impressed them with her knowledge, intelligence, and sense of humor.

She had never written for television before, but was very interested in doing the project. The producers asked Angelou for the name of her agent. She did not have an agent, but she gave them Jerry Purcell's name and told them he was her manager. After the interview, Angelou phoned Purcell and told him what she had done.

Three days later Purcell called Angelou and told her that he had negotiated a large sum of money for her to write and direct ten one-hour segments for television. Angelou would have to move to San Francisco for a month or so to film the project.

Though Angelou knew nothing about camera angles or equipment, she accepted the challenge. Before leaving New York, Angelou went to the library and read up on television terms and phrases. When she was not reading about television, she wrote the series, which she called, *Blacks, Blues, Black*.[6] Each segment told of another part of African-American culture and history in American life. Angelou intended to narrate the programs that would highlight many African-American traditions that are still current in American life. She wrote on topics from poetry and blues music to church choirs singing spirituals and gospel songs. Angelou, a trained dancer, also wanted to feature African-American modern dance, ballet, and art in her programs.

Several days before Angelou left for San Francisco, Robert Loomis, an editor from the publishing company Random House called. He had been given her name by Judy Feiffer. He asked Angelou if she was interested in writing her autobiography. She said no, and explained that she considered herself a poet and playwright.[7] Angelou also told him she was leaving New York in a few days to film her *Blacks, Blues, Black* series.

In San Francisco, Angelou went right to work assembling dancers, singers, musicians, and artists for her series. Robert Loomis called after her first day of shooting. He asked again if she would write her autobiography for Random House. Angelou told him no, but said she would be happy to speak with him about publishing a book of poetry when she returned to New York.

Soon Angelou's creativity, intellect, and organizational skills were in full swing. She received total cooperation from everyone she approached. Angelou was even able to borrow a full collection of valuable Makonde sculpture, indigenous to Africa, from Bishop Trevor Hoy at the Pacific School of Religion.

Blacks, Blues, Black received favorable reviews in the newspapers. Angelou's friends Rosa and Dolly came out from New York for the premiere. Angelou's mother was particularly proud of her.

"Yes I Can"

The minute someone tells Angelou that she cannot do something, her energy goes up and she says, "Yes I can." Angelou believes that "all things are possible for a human being." She believes there is nothing in the world she cannot do.[9]

On Angelou's last day in San Francisco, Robert Loomis called again. He told Angelou he was not going to bother her again. He explained to her that it is nearly impossible to write an autobiography as literature.[8] Just then Angelou said, "I'll do it."

The next day Angelou, Dolly, and Rosa traveled to Stockton, California, to visit Angelou's mother. The women laughed, ate, and told stories. Early one morning Angelou took out a yellow pad of paper. As she thought about how far African-American women had come from the days of slavery, she took notes for her book. Angelou wanted it to be about how the human spirit rises and triumphs above life's slights and defeats.[10] While she wrote, she remembered the poem "Sympathy," by Paul Lawrence Dunbar, from her mute days in Stamps, Arkansas. The poem begins, "*I know why the caged bird sings*, alas."

That line would become the title of Angelou's first autobiography. She would open with these sentences, "What you looking at me for? I didn't come to stay." It was Angelou's way of saying that no matter what you thought of her situation, she was headed for better days.[11]

Now Angelou was going back to New York, to write the story of her amazing, remarkable life.

Chapter 11

THE CAGED
BIRD SINGS

I n 1970, forty-two-year-old Angelou published *I Know
Why the Caged Bird Sings*, the first volume of her
autobiography. This book covers Angelou's life from
early childhood through her graduation from high school
and the birth of her son. Angelou's uplifting theme—
survival with dignity and courage in a hostile environment—
touched so many readers that she became the first African-
American woman to make the nonfiction bestseller list.

Honors and awards followed the success of her first book.
Angelou was appointed Poet in Residence at the University of
Kansas and named a Fellow at Yale University. Executives at
Columbia, a movie studio in Southern California, invited
Angelou to Hollywood to write a screenplay for Alex Haley's
book *The Autobiography of Malcolm X*. Learning that her
long-absent father had died was the only incident that flawed
her happiness during this time.

Although she had been writing poetry all her life, Angelou published her first volume of poetry, *Just Give Me a Cool Drink of Water 'Fore I Diie*, in 1971. After the book was nominated for a Pulitzer Prize, Angelou lectured at Wake Forest University in North Carolina, where she received the North Carolina Award for Literature. Six hundred students came to hear Angelou's talk. The audience became so excited that by the end of her lecture they were standing and calling out questions.[1]

In 1972, Angelou became the first African-American woman in the United States to write a Hollywood screenplay and have it produced. *Georgia, Georgia,* the story of two African-American women touring Sweden, deals with interracial relationships. She wrote the script to show African-American women as they really are. Multitalented Angelou also composed the musical score for the film. After *Georgia, Georgia* completed production in Sweden, Angelou returned there to study filmmaking.

Later that same year, Angelou, forty-four, met writer-cartoonist Paul Du Feu at a literary party in London. Angelou and Du Feu fell in love. They were married in 1973 at the multiracial Glide Community Church in San Francisco. Angelou and Du Feu lived in Los Angeles, then moved to the Sonoma Valley in Northern California.[2]

This was a happy period in Angelou's life.[3] In addition to writing and lecturing at California State University at Sacramento, Angelou spent many hours preparing gourmet meals. Angelou's passion for cooking inspired her to collect over one hundred cookbooks. Guy lived in San Francisco and stayed in close touch with his mother. During this time, Angelou became a grandmother to Guy's son, Colin Ashanti Murphy-Johnson.

Angelou also continued acting and in 1973 played Mary Todd Lincoln's dressmaker in the Broadway play *Look Away*. She received a Tony nomination for her performance. Her husband earned his living buying, restoring, and selling old homes around Sonoma Valley. But he often traveled with Angelou to her visiting professorships, acting gigs and screenwriting jobs. Even though she had a hectic work schedule, Angelou found time to plant a vegetable garden at their Sonoma Valley home. She insisted on sharing quiet meals at home with family or friends as often as possible.

Her next autobiographical book, *Gather Together in My Name*, took Angelou three years to write. Released in 1974, the book describes Angelou's efforts to overcome economic difficulties and her search for self-worth as a teenage mother. Angelou's strong spirit begins to emerge and she dares to dream of a better life in spite of her difficult circumstances.[4]

In 1975 President Gerald Ford appointed Angelou to the American Revolution Bicentennial Council. Angelou's grace with words continued in her poetry. After the publication of another book of poems, *Oh Pray My Wings Are Gonna Fit Me Well*, members of the Rockefeller Foundation picked Angelou to be one of fifteen scholars-in-residence at the Bellagio Study and Conference Center on Lake Como in Italy.

Angelou and Du Feu found the center luxurious and formal. One evening, during dinner, the director of the center asked if anyone had a good recipe for turkey and cornbread stuffing. Thanksgiving was coming up, and none of his staff had a recipe. Angelou volunteered cooking instructions for both. The next day, the director asked Angelou to go the kitchen because no one was able to follow her directions.

When the head chef saw Angelou, he let her know he had expected a white man to come to the kitchen and asked his assistant to speak with her.[5] Angelou rose above the insult and asked the assistant chef for cornmeal. Instead of the dry, crumbly cornmeal she was used to, Angelou was given polenta, a fine yellow Italian cornmeal soaked with water until it turned into mush. She had never cooked with polenta before. Next Angelou asked for baking powder, but no one in the kitchen had ever heard of it. Concerned but determined, she began chopping and mixing together ingredients.

After the turkey filled with cornbread stuffing came out of the oven, the head chef was so impressed he nodded his approval at her.[6] The guests applauded Angelou when dinner was served. But for Angelou there was a larger message than her perfect Thanksgiving turkey. She learned that food and its preparation could bridge distances between races, sexes, and languages.[7]

Angelou had worked on the third volume of her autobiography, *Sittin' and Swingin' and Gettin' Merry Like Christmas*, during her stay in Italy. The book begins with Angelou as a young unwed mother in San Francisco and ends with her return from Europe after performing in the musical *Porgy and Bess*. Angelou used her traveling experiences to show her respect for other cultures and how she could find joy in almost any situation. Following the book's 1976 release, Angelou and Du Feu went on a nationwide lecture and book promotion tour.

Over the next several years, Angelou directed two National Educational Television films. She also continued acting, receiving an Emmy nomination for her performance as Nyo Boto in Alex Haley's television miniseries *Roots*. In 1978 she released *And Still I Rise*, another volume of poetry.

Angelou continued to share her life's journey in the fourth volume of her autobiography, *The Heart of a Woman*, published in 1981. This book covers the period of her life when she worked as a political activist in New York up to her move to Ghana.

By now Angelou had become famous. But as Angelou's fame grew, her marriage began to falter. Angelou and Du Feu separated and divorced in 1981.[8] Soon after their separation, she was appointed lifetime Reynolds Professor of American Studies at Wake Forest University in North Carolina.

Angelou was not sure she wanted to move back to the South. She described the South as hard and mean.[9] But after much consideration, she bought a ten-room, redbrick, colonial-style house in Winston-Salem, North Carolina. Once she settled into her home, Angelou began collecting African art. As her collection grew, she needed more wall space to hang paintings. Over time she has had the house expanded to eighteen rooms.

Since 1982, Angelou has taught African-American literature and cultural history one semester a year at Wake Forest. This schedule allows her enough time to continue her writing. The rare books room of the university has the journals Angelou kept when she was a child.

By the time Angelou turned fifty-five and her book of poetry *Shaker, Why Don't You Sing?* came out, she was receiving more than three hundred fan letters a week. *All God's Children Need Travelin' Shoes*, the fifth volume of her autobiography, recounts her time in Ghana and her coming to terms with the issues of race and identity. Her book of poetry *Now Sheba Sings the Song*, published in 1987, received critical praise, as did *I Shall Not Be Moved*, another volume of her poetry published in 1990. Throughout her poetry and autobiographies Angelou describes not only what happened to her, but also life's effect on her.[10] Many readers identify with Angelou's response to life's challenges and her ability to take risks, and with the way she finds personal freedom in her heart.

Angelou had worked hard throughout the 1980s and achieved great professional success. In the early 1990s, her beloved mother became ill with cancer. Angelou had always admired her mother's beauty, toughness, and common sense. She moved her mother into her home to care for her. Vivian Baxter died in 1992.

That year had its happier moments too, including a trip to Washington, D.C., to receive the Horatio Alger Award. As a child, Angelou had enjoyed the works of Horatio Alger. He wrote stories about poor people who by hard work, honesty, and honorable intentions made great successes of their lives. Like the characters in Horatio Alger's novels, Angelou had fashioned her success from such qualities.

Talking to a Full House

When Angelou is not teaching at Wake Forest University, she travels around the United States lecturing to sold-out audiences. Her presentations range in content from poetry to songs to stories and back again. No matter how Angelou begins her talk, she ends the evening by telling her audience that courage is the greatest virtue—"because without courage, you can't practice any other virtue consistently."[11]

One evening Angelou told an audience in San Diego, California, that she has learned that "human beings are more alike than unalike" and that all people must refuse the hardening of the human spirit and stay open to one another. Only then will people be able to live together in peace.[12]

Chapter 12

A NATIONAL TREASURE

On a fall morning in 1992, Angelou had received a call from president-elect Bill Clinton. The future forty-second president of the United States asked Angelou to compose and read a poem for his inauguration. Robert Frost, who had spoken at the inauguration of President John F. Kennedy in 1960, was the first poet to read a poem at the inauguration of a United States president. Maya Angelou became only the second poet and the first African-American woman to do so.[1]

Angelou knew that composing a poem for this historic event would be a great challenge. Determined to do well and fortified by her strong work ethic, Angelou went into high gear. She studied and read works by the abolitionist Frederick Douglas, scholar W.E.B. Du Bois, and poet Frances Ellen Watkins Harper to prepare for writing the poem.[2] Angelou also followed the working pattern she had come to prefer: She took a hotel room and told the staff not to disturb her. The bed would not be used, she said, so the sheets did not have to be changed. Angelou took along a Bible, a dictionary, *Roget's Thesaurus*, a bottle of sherry, plus a deck of cards to play the card game solitaire.

Each morning she arrived at the hotel by 5:30 A.M. and wrote and rewrote on yellow legal pads until two in the afternoon. After a short lunch break, Angelou began writing again. She often she worked until late at night. Though "On the Pulse of Morning" contained only 650 words, by the time Angelou finished composing the inaugural poem she had filled more than two hundred handwritten pages.

Welcoming a President

President Clinton chose Angelou because her life's work—her poetry and five autobiographical volumes—used words to bring people together. Angelou writes from an African-American point of view, but her work goes beyond the boundaries of race to show how people are more alike than different.[3]

On the morning of January 20, 1993, Angelou eloquently read her poem "On the Pulse of Morning" in front of the hundreds gathered in Washington, D.C., for the inauguration of President Clinton. Thousands more listened to her majestic voice on their radios, while millions more watched the inaugural event on television. Angelou's poem encouraged people everywhere to have hope for the future even though the past has been difficult. President Clinton hugged Angelou when she finished. "I loved your poem," he said.[3] Loud cheers and a standing ovation thundered through Washington, across the country, and around the world.

When Angelou turned sixty-five in 1993, her close friend Oprah Winfrey hosted a party on a cruise ship. Celebrities from all over the world came to Angelou's birthday celebration. Oprah commented that each person invited thought they were Angelou's closest friend.[5] Angelou dedicated her book *Wouldn't Take Nothing for My Journey Now* to Oprah Winfrey "with immeasurable love."[6]

In following her own unique artistic path, Maya Angelou has become one of the most respected literary figures in the last half of the twentieth century. She remained productive through the 1990s. Between 1994 and 1997 she published five books, including two children's books, *My Painted House, My Friendly Chicken and Me* (1994) and *Kofi and His Magic* (1996).

In the sixth volume of Angelou's autobiography, *A Song Flung Up to Heaven*, released in 2002, she details with humor and courage the period of her life when she returns from Ghana through her work for Dr. King, helping him organize the Poor People's March. The book ends after Dr. King is assassinated and tells how her close friend James Baldwin helped her find her voice to begin writing her autobiography.

Oprah Winfrey had once asked Angelou to write a cookbook. In 2004, Angelou published, *Hallelujah! The Welcome Table: A Lifetime of Memories with Recipes*. This large, beautifully photographed book combines the two things Angelou enjoys most: cooking and writing. Angelou considers herself a serious cook.[7] She is often asked to cook in competitions for events to raise money for charities supporting cancer research, sickle-cell anemia—a hereditary blood disease more common among African Americans—and the American Jewish Association. People pay up to $250 to eat her food.

On December 1, 2005, Dr. Angelou read her Christmas poem "Amazing Peace" at the lighting of the National Christmas Tree at the White House. Several months later, when her good friend Coretta Scott King passed away, Maya Angelou delivered a eulogy at Mrs. King's memorial service.

Through her writing, lectures, and teaching Angelou's message remains consistent: People must work to overcome their hardships with dignity and view the world with hope and love.[8]

These days, when Angelou speaks to an audience the stage set often resembles a living room. The poet speaks to the group as if they are gathered in her home and she knows them personally, using songs, poetry, funny stories, and political anecdotes. Audiences all over the United States have listened to Angelou share her belief that once people accept themselves, they will realize the worthiness of all people.

Angelou has lived life taking risks and learning from her mistakes. Her strong work ethic and deep religious beliefs have helped her rise to meet all of life's challenges. But as a great writer, Angelou's use of words to create a kinder, more peaceful world is what makes her a national treasure.[9]

CHRONOLOGY

1928—Marguerite Johnson is born April 4 in St. Louis, Missouri.

1931—Marguerite, now called Maya, and her brother, Bailey, are sent to Stamps, Arkansas, to live with their grandmother Annie Henderson.

1940—Maya and Bailey move to their mother's home in California.

1944—Maya works as a conductor on a cable car.

1945—Graduates from Mission High School in San Francisco. Son Clyde (later called Guy) is born.

1952—Marries Tosh Angelos.

1953—Begins performing at the Purple Onion nightclub in San Francisco. Takes the name Maya Angelou.

1954—Tours Europe with traveling theater company performing *Porgy and Bess.*

1955—Moves to New York City with son Guy and joins the Harlem Writers Guild.

1960—Produces *Cabaret for Freedom.* Works for the Southern Christian Leadership Conference (SCLC). Marries freedom fighter Vusumzi Make. Performs off-Broadway in Jean Genet's play *The Blacks.*

1961—Moves to Cairo, Egypt, with husband and son.

1962—Takes job as associate editor at *The Arab Observer.* Divorces Make. Moves to Ghana.

1965—Writes articles for the *Ghanaian Times* and the Ghanaian Broadcasting Company.

1968—Writes *Blacks, Blues, Black* for National Educational Television.

1970—*I Know Why the Caged Bird Sings*, the first book in her autobiographical series, is published and nominated for the National Book Award.

1971—Her first volume of poetry, *Just Give Me a Cool Drink of Water 'Fore I Diie*, is published.

1972—Nominated for a Pulitzer Prize. Writes, directs, and produces original screenplay, *Georgia, Georgia*.

1973—Marries Paul Du Feu.

1974—Publishes second autobiography, *Gather Together in My Name*. Becomes visiting professor at three colleges: Wake Forest University, Wichita State University, and California State University at Sacramento.

1975—*Oh Pray My Wings Are Gonna Fit Me Well*, second book of poems, is published. Is selected to be a Rockefeller Foundation Scholar and goes to Italy.

1976—*Singin' and Swingin and Gettin' Merry Like Christmas*, third volume of her autobiography, is published.

1978—Publishes *And Still I Rise*, her third book of poetry.

1981—*The Heart of a Woman*, fourth volume of autobiography, is published. Is divorced from Paul Du Feu.

1982—Appointed the Reynolds Chair in American Studies at Wake Forest University in Winston-Salem, North Carolina. Writes *Sister, Sister*, a teleplay for NBC-TV.

1983—*Shaker, Why Don't You Sing?*, her fourth book of poems, is published.

1986—*All God's Children Need Travelin' Shoes*, fifth volume of autobiography, is published.

1987—*Now Sheba Sing the Song*, fifth book of poems, is published.

1990—*I Shall Not Be Moved*, sixth book of poems, is published.

1992—Chosen by president-elect Bill Clinton to compose a poem for his inauguration ceremony.

1993—Reads her poem at President Clinton's inauguration. *Wouldn't Take Nothing for My Journey Now*, another autobiography, is published.

1994—*My Painted House, My Friendly Chicken and Me* and *The Complete Collected Poems of Maya Angelou* are published.

1995—Reads "A Brave and Startling Truth" at the fiftieth anniversary of the United Nations.

2002—*A Song Flung Up to Heaven*, seventh volume of her autobiography, is published.

2004—*Hallelujah! The Welcome Table: A Lifetime of Memories with Recipes* is published.

Works by Maya Angelou

Autobiographies

I Know Why the Caged Bird Sings, 1970
Gather Together in My Name, 1974
Singin' and Swingin' and Gettin' Merry Like Christmas, 1976
The Heart of a Woman, 1981
All God's Children Need Travelin' Shoes, 1986
Wouldn't Take Nothing for My Journey Now, 1993
Even the Stars Look Lonesome, 1997
A Song Flung Up to Heaven, 2002
Hallelujah! The Welcome Table: A Lifetime of Memories with Recipes, 2004

Books of Poetry

Just Give Me a Cool Drink of Water 'Fore I Diie, 1971
Oh Pray My Wings Are Gonna Fit Me Well, 1975
And Still I Rise, 1978
Shaker, Why Don't You Sing?, 1983
Now Sheba Sings the Song, 1987
I Shall Not Be Moved, 1990
The Complete Collected Poems of Maya Angelou, 1994
Phenomenal Woman: Four Poems for Women, 1995

Recordings

Miss Calypso (recorded songs), 1957, 1996
The Poetry of Maya Angelou, 1969
Maya Angelou (sound recording), 1978

Dramatic Works

Cabaret for Freedom (drama cowritten with
Godfrey Cambridge), 1960
The Least of These, 1966
Georgia, Georgia (screenplay), 1972
The Sisters (television screen play), 1978
On a Southern Journey, 1983

Children's Books

Life Doesn't Frighten Me, 1993
My Painted House, My Friendly Chicken and Me, 1994
Kofi and His Magic, 1996

Poems

"On the Pulse of Morning" (poem for Bill Clinton's presidential
inauguration), 1993
"A Brave and Startling Truth," 1995
"Amazing Peace, A Christmas Poem," 2005

Chapter Notes

Chapter 1. In the Spotlight

1. Lyman B. Hagen, *Heart of a Woman, Mind of a Writer and Soul of a Poet: A Critical Analysis of the Writings of Maya Angelou* (Lanham: University Press of America, 1997), p. 78.

2. Dolly A. McPherson, *Order Out of Chaos: The Autobiographical Works of Maya Angelou* (London: Virago Press, 1991), p. 77.

3. Maya Angelou, *Gather Together in My Name* (New York: Random House, 1974), p. 119.

4. Ibid., p. 126.

5. "An Intimate Evening with Maya Angelou," Smart Talk Women's Lecture Series, San Diego Civic Theater, May 12, 2004.

6. Ibid.

Chapter 2. Difficult Years

1. Jeffrey Elliott, *Conversations with Maya Angelou* (Jackson: University Press of Mississippi, 1989), p. 75.

2. Richard Wormser, *The Rise and Fall of Jim Crow* (New York: St. Martin's Press, 2003), p. 64.

3. Richard Baudouin, *Ku Klux Klan: A History of Racism and Violence* (Montgomery, Ala.: Southern Poverty Law Center, 1997), pp. 10, 12.

4. Mary E. Williams, ed., *Readings on Maya Angelou* (San Diego: Greenhaven Press, 1997), p. 106.

5. Dolly A. McPherson, *Order Out of Chaos: The Autobiographical Works of Maya Angelou* (London: Virago Press, 1991), pp. 81–82.

6. Lyman B. Hagen, *Heart of a Woman, Mind of a Writer and Soul of a Poet: A Critical Analysis of the Writings of Maya Angelou* (Lanham: University Press of America, 1997), p. 67.

7. McPherson, pp. 27–28.

8. Ibid., p. 38.

9. Maya Angelou, *I Know Why the Caged Bird Sings* (New York: Random House, 1970), p. 60.

10. Williams, p. 16.

11. McPherson, p. 40.

12. Hilton Als, *The New Yorker*, August 5, 2002, p. 72.

13. Williams, p. 17.

14. Hagen, p. 62.

15. McPherson, p. 42.

16. Williams, p. 17.

17. McPherson, p. 42.

18. Angelou, p. 99.

19. Williams, p. 58.

20. Ibid., p. 56.

Chapter 3. Days of Change

1. Dolly A. McPherson, *Order Out of Chaos: The Autobiographical Works of Maya Angelou* (London: Virago Press, 1991), p. 33.

2. Ibid., p. 33.

3. Maya Angelou, *I Know Why the Caged Bird Sings* (New York: Random House, 1970), p. 203.

4. McPherson, p. 50.

5. Jeffrey Elliott, *Conversations with Maya Angelou* (Jackson: University Press of Mississippi, 1989), p. 121.

6. Tonettte Bond Inge, *Southern Women Writers: The New Generation* (Tuscaloosa: University of Alabama Press, 1990), p. 120.

7. Lawson Fusao Wakida, *Only What We Could Carry*, (Berkeley, Ca.: Heyday Books, 1998), p. xii.

8. Lyman B. Hagen, *Heart of a Woman, Mind of a Writer and Soul of a Poet: A Critical Analysis of the Writings of Maya Angelou* (Lanham: University Press of America, 1997), p. 68.

9. Mary E. Williams, ed., *Readings on Maya Angelou* (San Diego: Greenhaven Press, 1997), pp. 17–18.

10. Ibid., p. 18.

11. Angelou, p. 288.

12. Wendalyn R. Nichols, ed., Random House Webster's Dictionary (New York: Random House, 1990), p. 97.

13. McPherson, p. 82.

14. Hagen, p. 89.

15. Williams, p. 19.

16. Ibid., p. 20.

17. Maya Angelou, *Singin' and Swingin' and Gettin' Merry Like Christmas* (New York: Random House, 1976), p. 51.

18. Tonettte Bond Inge, *Southern Women Writers: The New Generation* (Tuscaloosa: University of Alabama Press, 1990), p. 123.

19. Ibid., p. 123.

Chapter 4. New Paths

1. Maya Angelou, *Singin' and Swingin' and Gettin' Merry Like Christmas* (New York: Random House, 1976), p. 106.

2. Mary E. Williams, ed., *Readings on Maya Angelou* (San Diego: Greenhaven Press, 1997), p. 20.

3. Angelou, p. 110.

4. Lyman B. Hagen, *Heart of a Woman, Mind of a Writer and Soul of a Poet: A Critical Analysis of the Writings of Maya Angelou* (Lanham: University Press of America, 1997), p. 90.

5. Dolly A. McPherson, *Order Out of Chaos: The Autobiographical Works of Maya Angelou* (London: Virago Press, 1991), p. 89.

6. Ibid., p. 85.

7. Ibid., p. 89.

8. Iain McLean and Alistair McMillan, *Oxford Concise Dictionary of Politics* (Oxford: Oxford University Press, 2003), p. 88.

9. Hagen, p. 93.

10. McLean, p. 87.

11. Tonettte Bond Inge, *Southern Women Writers: The New Generation* (Tuscaloosa: University of Alabama Press, 1990), p. 125.

12. Jeffrey Elliott, *Conversations with Maya Angelou* (Jackson: University Press of Mississippi, 1989), p. 47.

13. Maya Angelou, *Singin' and Swingin' and Gettin' Merry Like Christmas* (New York: Random House, 1976), p. 288.

14. Inge, p. 127.

15. Elliott, p. 36.

Chapter 5. On Her Way

1. Lyman B. Hagen, *Heart of a Woman, Mind of a Writer and Soul of a Poet: A Critical Analysis of the Writings of Maya Angelou* (Lanham: University Press of America, 1997), p. 102.

2. Dolly A. McPherson, *Order Out of Chaos: The Autobiographical Works of Maya Angelou* (London: Virago Press, 1991), p. 91.

3. Mary E. Williams, ed., *Readings on Maya Angelou* (San Diego: Greenhaven Press, 1997), p. 21.

4. Maya Angelou, *The Heart of a Woman*, (New York: Random House, 1981), p. 51.

5. Sanford Wexler, *The Civil Rights Movement* (New York: Facts On File, Inc., 1999), p. ix.

6. Ibid., pp. 89–90.

7. Ibid., p. 74.

8. Iain McLean and Alistair McMillan, *Oxford Concise Dictionary of Politics* (Oxford: Oxford University Press, 2003), p. 294.

9. Williams, p. 22.

10. McPherson, p. 92.

11. Tonettte Bond Inge, *Southern Women Writers: The New Generation* (Tuscaloosa: University of Alabama Press, 1990), p. 127.

12. Williams, p. 22.

13. Ibid., p. 23.

14. Ibid.

15. Inge, p. 127.

Chapter 6. Exotic Adventures

1. Tonettte Bond Inge, *Southern Women Writers: The New Generation* (Tuscaloosa: University of Alabama Press, 1990), p. 127.

2. Dolly A. McPherson, *Order Out of Chaos: The Autobiographical Works of Maya Angelou* (London: Virago Press, 1991), p. 98.

3. Mary E. Williams, ed., *Readings on Maya Angelou* (San Diego: Greenhaven Press, 1997), p. 92.

4. McPherson, p. 98.

5. Lyman B. Hagen, *Heart of a Woman, Mind of a Writer and Soul of a Poet: A Critical Analysis of the Writings of Maya Angelou* (Lanham: University Press of America, 1997), p. 106.

6. James H. Cone, *Martin & Malcolm & America: A Dream or a Nightmare* (New York: Orbis Books, 1992), p. 311.

7. Iain McLean and Alistair McMillan, *Oxford Concise Dictionary of Politics* (Oxford: Oxford University Press, 2003), p. 220.

8. Jeffrey Elliott, *Conversations with Maya Angelou* (Jackson: University Press of Mississippi, 1989), p. 160.

9. Linda Fasulo, *An Insider's Guide to the UN* (New Haven, Conn.: Yale University Press, 2004), pp. 1, 3.

10. McPherson, p. 94.

11. Williams, p. 135.

12. Elliott, p. 72.

13. McPherson, pp. 99–98.

14. Ibid., p. 99.

15. Williams, p. 92.

16. Wendalyn R. Nichols, ed., *Random House Webster's Dictionary* (New York: Random House, 1990), p. 950.

Chapter 7. Seeking Her Heritage

1. Jerry Cohen and William S. Murphy, *Burn Baby Burn!* (New York: Dutton & Co., Inc. 1996), p. 8.

2. Sanford Wexler, *The Civil Rights Movement* (New York: Facts On File, Inc., 1999), pp. 169, 195.

3. Mary E. Williams, ed., *Readings on Maya Angelou* (San Diego: Greenhaven Press, 1997), p. 24.

4. Ibid., p. 24.

5. Sanford Wexler, *The Civil Rights Movement* (New York: Facts On File, Inc., 1999), p. 310.

6. Iain McLean and Alistair McMillan, *Oxford Concise Dictionary of Politics* (Oxford: Oxford University Press, 2003), p. 391.

7. Maya Angelou, *All God's Children Need Travelin' Shoes* (New York: Random House, 1986), p. 18.

8. Lyman B. Hagen, *Heart of a Woman, Mind of a Writer and Soul of a Poet: A Critical Analysis of the Writings of Maya Angelou* (Lanham: University Press of America, 1997), pp. 106–107.

9. Williams, p. 93.

10. Jeffrey Elliott, *Conversations with Maya Angelou* (Jackson: University Press of Mississippi, 1989), p. 157.

11. Williams, p. 25.

12. Ibid., p. 25.

13. Clayton Carson, *Malcolm X: The FBI File* (New York: Carroll & Graf Publishers, Inc., 1991), p. 327.

14. Ibid., p. 328.

15. Angelou, p. 195.

Chapter 8. Wandering

1. Maya Angelou, *All God's Children Need Travelin' Shoes* (New York: Random House, 1991), p. 199.

2. Ibid.

3. Jeffrey Elliott, *Conversations with Maya Angelou* (Jackson: University Press of Mississippi, 1989), p. 33.

4. Maya Angelou, *A Song Flung Up to Heaven* (New York: Random House, 2002), p. 20.

5. Lyman B. Hagen, *Heart of a Woman, Mind of a Writer and Soul of a Poet: A Critical Analysis of the Writings of Maya Angelou* (Lanham: University Press of America, 1997), p. 107.

6. Mary E. Williams, ed., *Readings on Maya Angelou* (San Diego: Greenhaven Press, 1997), p. 25.

7. Ibid., p. 94.

8. Clayton Carson, *Malcolm X: The FBI File* (New York: Carroll & Graf Publishers, Inc., 1991), p. 83.

9. Ibid., p. 396.

10. Angelou, p. 49.

11. Elliott, p. 33.

Chapter 9. Finding Meaning

1. Robert Conot, *Rivers of Blood, Years of Darkness* (New York: William Morrow and Company, Inc., 1968), p. 4.

2. Jerry Cohen and William S. Murphy, *Burn Baby Burn!* (New York: Dutton & Co., 1996), pp. 65, 67.

3. Maya Angelou, *A Song Flung Up to Heaven* (New York: Random House, 2002), p. 68.

4. Conot, pp. ix–x.

5. Cohen and Murphy, p. 290.

6. Ibid., pp. 312–313.

7. Jeffrey Elliott, *Conversations with Maya Angelou* (Jackson: University Press of Mississippi, 1989), p. 33.

8. Angelou, p. 119.

9. Ibid., p. 181.

10. Ibid., p. 173.

Chapter 10. In Full Swing

1. Maya Angelou, *A Song Flung Up to Heaven* (New York: Random House, 2002), p. 187.

2. Ibid., p. 189.

3. James H. Cone, *Martin & Malcolm & America: A Dream or a Nightmare* (New York: Orbis Books, 1992), pp. 288–289.

4. Maya Angelou, *A Song Flung Up to Heaven* (New York: Random House, 2002), p. 193.

5. Lyman B. Hagen, *Heart of a Woman, Mind of a Writer and Soul of a Poet: A Critical Analysis of the Writings of Maya Angelou* (Lanham: University Press of America, 1997), p. 56.

6. Ibid., p. 142.

7. Jeffrey Elliott, *Conversations with Maya Angelou* (Jackson: University Press of Mississippi, 1989), p. 191.

8. Ibid., p. 211.

9. Dolly A. McPherson, *Order Out of Chaos The Autobiographical Works of Maya Angelou* (London: Virago Press, 1991), p. 22.

10. Ibid., p. 129.

11. Ibid., p. 24.

Chapter 11. The Caged Bird Sings

1. Jeffrey Elliott, *Conversations with Maya Angelou* (Jackson: University Press of Mississippi, 1989), p. 209.

2. Ibid., p. 75.

3. Ibid., p. 35.

4. Mary E. Williams, ed., *Readings on Maya Angelou* (San Diego: Greenhaven Press, 1997), p. 70.

5. Maya Angelou, *Hallelujah! The Welcome Table* (New York: Random House, 2004), p. 114.

6. Ibid., p. 115.

7. Ibid., p. 116.

8. Elliott, p. 128.

9. Maya Angelou, "Why I Moved Back to the South," *Ebony,* February 1982, pp. 130–131.

10. Tonettte Bond Inge, *Southern Women Writers: The New Generation* (Tuscaloosa: University of Alabama Press, 1990), p. 117.

11. Ibid.

12. Karima A. Hazynes, "Maya Angelou: Prime Time Poet," *Ebony,* April 1993, p. 72.

Chapter 12. A National Treasure

1. Lucinda Moore, "A Conversation with Maya Angelou," Smithsonian, April 2003, p. 96.

2. Karima A. Hazynes, "Maya Angelou: Prime Time Poet," *Ebony,* April 1993, p. 70.

3. Ibid., p. 73.

4. Ibid., p. 72.

5. "Oprah Throws a Party," *Ebony,* June 1993, pp. 119–120.

6. "An Intimate Evening with Maya Angelou," Smart Talk Women's Lecture Series, San Diego Civic Theater, May 12, 2004.

7. Jeffrey Elliott, *Conversations with Maya Angelou* (Jackson: University Press of Mississippi, 1989), p. 215.

8. "An Intimate Evening with Maya Angelou," Smart Talk Women's Lecture Series, San Diego Civic Theater, May 12, 2004.

9. Margaret Courtney-Clark, *Maya Angelou: The Poetry of Living* (New York: Clarkson Potter, 1999), p. 126.

FURTHER READING AND INTERNET ADDRESSES

Books

Angelou, Maya. *I Know Why the Caged Bird Sings.* New York, NY: Random House Publishers Group, Inc., 2009.

Egan, Jill. *Maya Angelou: A Creative and Courageous Voice.* York, PA: Gareth Stevens Publishing, 2009.

Johnson, Claudia. *Racism in Maya Angelou's I Know Why the Caged Bird Sings.* San Diego, CA: Greenhaven, 2007.

Kite, L. Patricia. *Maya Angelou.* Minneapolis, MN: Lerner Publications Company, 2006.

Naden, Corinne and Rose Blue. *Maya Angelou.* Mankato, MN: Heinemann-Raintree, 2005.

Internet Addresses

Maya Angelou
This is the official web site for Maya Angelou
<http://mayaangelou.com/>

Biography.Com
Read a biography of Maya Angelou—Facts, Birthday and Life story.
<http://www.biography.com/people/maya-angelou-9185388>

INDEX